Joe Brumbelow was one of a [...] able wherever he was—with [...] His faithfulness in ministry is typified by [...] commitment that he demonstrated throughout his ministry to the Lord. His sense of humor was contagious and his seriousness about the things that really counted was remarkable. You will enjoy these pages and be greatly blessed by them. I'm happy to commend this book.

> —James T. Draper, President
> LifeWay Christian Resources, Nashville, TN

David Brumbelow's book, *The Wit and Wisdom of Pastor Joe Brumbelow*, is a welcome addition to all who knew Joe Brumbelow. All of his ministry, he was more reliable than Old Faithful and could always be depended on to do what was right, to believe all that was necessary, and to bring fun to everyone involved. David Brumbelow has captured some of the best from his father. Even those who did not know Joe Brumbelow will now have the opportunity to be blessed by his life and ministry.

> —Paige Patterson, President
> Southwestern Baptist Theological Seminary, Fort Worth, TX

Delightful reading of this book will refresh, teach, and inspire God's people. Joe's quiet, fun-filled life joined with his extreme love of Jesus and people will bless those who read. We are enriched to have it available.

> —Franklin Atkinson, Th.D.
> Longtime Bible professor at East Texas Baptist University
> Marshall, TX

Pastors tell stories because pastors see stories every day. And people love to hear stories, especially those that lighten or strengthen their hearts. David Brumbelow shares such stories, observations, and anecdotes he recalls from his dad, and in so doing, lightens and strengthens the heart of the reader. You will enjoy the warmth and emotion that permeate the pages as David allows you to know his dad in a fun and inspirational way. If you're a pastor, you especially will love the book, because you will relate to so many of the experiences. I recommend the *The Wit and Wisdom of Pastor Joe Brumbelow*.

> —H. Edwin Young, Pastor
> Second Baptist Church, Houston, Texas

Printed in the United States of America
by Lightning Source, LaVergne, Tennessee
Cover design by Greg Crull
Except where otherwise indicated, Scripture taken
from the *New King James Version*. Copyright 1979, 1980, 1982
by Thomas Nelson, Inc. Used by permission. All rights reserved.
Library of Congress Control Number: 2005923907
ISBN 0-929292-62-6
Contact the author by writing:
David R. Brumbelow, P.O. Box 300, Lake Jackson, Texas 77566.

Permission granted to use brief excerpts if followed by
The Wit and Wisdom of Pastor Joe Brumbelow,
hannibalbooks.com

Hannibal Books
P.O. Box 461592
Garland, Texas 75046
1-800-747-0738
www.hannibalbooks.com

Front cover photos (clockwise, from left): Joe Brumbelow, 1951; Joe Brumbelow, 1938; Brother Joe baptizing Clem Lundie, Doverside Baptist Church, Houston, TX, 1971; Joe with speckled trout he caught at Texas Baptist Encampment, Palacios, TX. Background photo: Cotton field just south of Damon, TX. Back cover photo: Joe Brumbelow, June, 2002; Damon, TX, cotton field.

THE WIT AND WISDOM

of

PASTOR JOE BRUMBELOW

*Favorite illustrations, personal stories, humor, history, folklore,
and lessons learned from over 50 years in the ministry*

by his son,

DAVID R. BRUMBELOW

HANNIBAL BOOKS
www.hannibalbooks.com

Dedicated to:

Those in this life and the next who have been faithful members of the churches in which Brother Joe served. Nothing is more encouraging to a pastor than to have faithful, giving members on whom pastors can count in good times and bad.

The many preachers, evangelists, missionaries, and staff members who were his personal friends.

First Baptist Church of Lake Jackson, TX, for its love and support of Brother Joe when he served there, and for its love and support of his family when he went to be with the Lord.

All those who attended the memorial service, sent cards, sent flowers, called, visited, brought food, and have shown so many acts of Christian kindness.

Those who have since expressed to Bonnie, Steve, Mark, and David so many wonderful comments about what Joe Brumbelow meant to them. What a privilege to be a part of the family of God!

For God is not unrighteous to forget your work and labour of love, which ye have shewed toward his name, in that ye have ministered to the saints, and do minister (Heb. 6:10 KJV).

Acknowledgements

Special thanks to—
• Mrs. Dorothy Salser, pianist and English teacher, who proofread this book. She agreed to do so in spite of my desire to keep the book informal and written much the same way as I and others would speak. She helped tremendously; the errors that are left are mine.
• others who proofread and made helpful comments: John and Alice Hatch, Bonnie Brumbelow, Mark and Cherry Brumbelow, Steve and Nelda Brumbelow, Bill and Lavinia (Bonnie) Brumbelow, Myrtle Mae (Brumbelow) Montier, and Micah Joseph Brumbelow.
• Louis and Kay Moore of Hannibal Books for their editing and helpful comments.
• Jack Cone of Highlands, TX, for use of his Global Positioning System (GPS).

Table of Contents

What a Well-Behaved Boy!; Forgiveness and Qualifications or
Shooting Our Wounded; Preaching and Politics; Tobacco; Some
Favorite Songs; What Then?; Father Brumbelow?; Deacons;
Stranded on Uninhabited Isle; Best Thing a Father Can Do for His
Children Is to Love Their Mother; What a Great Testimony; Two
Ph.D's; World War II Hero, Sinner, Saint; One Evening in October;
Practical Jokes; Study Bibles; Red-Letter Edition; Identity of the
Antichrist; The Day Joe Brumbelow Lost His Faith; Preachers and
Fried Chicken; Brother Joe.

Redeemed; The Old Preacher; The Biggest Lie; Churchill and the
Cup of Tea; Growing Up in the Hill Country; Running with a
Walking Cane; Leaving the SBC; Ramblers and Cadillacs;
Honeybees; Humility; Simon Peter and Racism; A Spiritual Nap;
Broken Record; Jesus Paid a Part?; Greek and the Holy Land; How
to Have Revival; Bad Evangelists; Why Doesn't Pastor Snodgrass
Get Me to Preach?; The Blessing; Christmas Lights; Soul-Winning
Is What It's All About; The Infallible Word; Communism; I Think
Jesus Was a Good Man, a Great Teacher; Praise God!; Sad Case of
the Waders; Sleeping In Church; Insomnia; Don't Believe
Everything You Read, or Even See; Guarantee Against Alcoholism;
Internet Links; Basics of the Christian Life.

Fire and Wildfire; Where She Belonged; Only a Sinner;
Crawfishing; When Joe Got Saved; Mrs. Lartigue and the
Mormons; Mrs. Stephens and the Jehovah's Witnesses; Runaway
Donkey in Downtown Damon; Careful Who You Goose; Fact,
Faith, Feelings; Answered Prayer; A Nickel on the Sidewalk; The
B.C.; It Didn't Work, Did It?; I Knew You Were a Hard Master;
Life Is Like; I'm Ahead; The Nuns; Biggest Industry; Getting Over
It; It Was So Cold . . .; Emotion vs. Faithfulness; Funeral, I Mean
Wedding.

The Gideon Speaker; Give Him Another Chance; Crooked Rows;
Hospital Exercise; Quakers and Baptists; Empty Bottles; Gardening
in Bad Soil; Gold in the Hollow Tree; Spitting Over Your Chin;

Motto; Decent Swim Suits?; How About a Coke®?; Bad Food at UCC; My Toe's On Fire!; Speaking of Toes . . .; Living What You Preach with Grandkids; Rat Now; Humor That Can't Be Corrected; Poetry I Thought Dad Must Have Written; Joe Under the Desk; Halloween and Outhouses; Y2K Panic; Fruit Trees Joe Grew; Tomatoes; Faith?; That's Too Spiritual; Expositors of the Bible; The Girl Who Saved His Ministry.

written by Mrs. Joe E. (Bonnie) Brumbelow
The Preacher's Wife; I Married the Preacher; Living with the Preacher

Trapping; Annuity Board; Honey, Let Me Take It for a Spin; Of Buzzards and Christians; Good Buddy, Please Help Me, I'm Burning; Odds and Ends; Lose Them to the Cause, or Lose the Cause to Them; Menudo or Jesus?; Seeking After a Sign; Say That Again?; Airplanes Over Damon; Healing Powers of the Seventh Son; Grandpa—Indians, Bear Hunting, Catfishing; Bears and Fur Trade in Early Texas; Martin Van Buren Brumbelow; Scared By a Bear; Toilets, Outdoor and Indoor; Preaching Along the Same Lines; Streaker in the Old Folks' Home; The German Spy; What a Pastor Needs; Advantage I Never Had; Barbers and Marriage; Comments on Joe Brumbelow by Older Sister Myrtle Mae Montier.

Good God, They Shot Grandma!; Bob Thrift and TV; Six Abreast; Charbon and Dipping Vats; Those Folks Have Got It Made; Thank You Lord, But . . .; Burr Oaks and Shotgun Shells; Right or Wrong?; When the Lord Leads; Insert Where Needed; How's Virginia Doing?; A Loving God Wouldn't Send Anyone to Hell; It Was the Governor; The Other Side Of the Cemetery; Sam Houston Teaches a Preacher a Thing or Two; I Know That's in the Bible; Floundering at Midnight; A Nickel in the Hand.

Change; Three Letters; Worthy Is the Lamb; Uncle Ben Price; A Canoe, A Barge, and the Intercoastal Canal; Bulls and Quail; Sam Houston's Conversion and Its Results; Small Treble Hooks; Ed

Young for President; Designer Jewels; Phat Physicians; Skunks, Boots, and the Schoolhouse Furnace; Right Foot, Left Foot; Attempted Murder of a School Teacher; Lying or a Bad Memory; Running Those Hogs off the Cliff; Accumulation of Wealth Does Not Bring Happiness; Most Preachers Are Honest, but . . . ; The Youth Evangelist; A Church Can Get Ripped Off; Football and Homeruns; And the Name Is . . .; A Motorcycle Gang Funeral; A Hook in the Ear.

Of Geese and Storms; Too Poor Not to Tithe; Denying Me a Blessing; How I Know the Bible Is God's Word; There Is a Time, I Know Not When; Arctic Circle; Mother's Day; Uncle Charlie; Fiddlers Island; Outdoor Stories; Ham and Ramsey; Born in Another World; Never Again; UFO's, Dreams, and Weird Occurrences ; Don't Blow A Moral Fuse; Sour Dirt in Damon; Helping Young Preachers; Cast Your Bread upon the Waters; God Uses Poverty.

The Robin to the Sparrow; Three Greek Scholars?; Papa George; To Whom Are You Talking?; A Confirmed Agnostic Meets Jesus; Can't Wait to Look in the Mirror; The Lord Loves a Cheerful Giver; Committees; A Problem of the Heart; LJ Minister Dies While Fishing; Why Three Kids?; Revival; To All Interested and Uninterested People; About a Preacher's Retirement; Getting in the Emergency Room; Youthful Mishaps; The Outhouse; The Passing of the Outhouse; The Hairdryer; A Man from Scotland Gets Saved; That's My Savior!; God Saves the Best For Last

Foreword

In the following pages you will read a moving tribute from a devoted son to a loving father. David Brumbelow, son of Pastor Joe Brumbelow, has captured the essence of his father's spirit and life. His deep love and profound respect for his father shines through every page. With humorous and inspiring anecdotes from his father's pastoral experiences woven with stories of personal and family life, David presents one of the most winsome and colorful personalities you will ever meet. Joe Brumbelow was a warm and tenderhearted person, a faithful and compassionate pastor, a devoted husband and father, and a genuine soldier of the cross. He dearly loved his family, his friends, and the churches he so faithfully served.

You will enjoy this book. Some of the funniest stories you will ever read are contained in the pages of this volume. As I read these stories, I laughed. You will laugh, too. You will laugh out loud. No other Baptist preacher managed to see the humor in so many situations of life. For almost five years Brother Joe served as the minister of pastoral care at First Baptist Church of Lake Jackson, TX. One day Brother Joe said to me, "Pastor, you've never told our staff what your expectations are in the event of a hurricane. Do you want us to stay and minister or to evacuate? What would you like for us to do?" I replied, "Brother Joe, I'll answer you like this. When Hurricane Alicia was parked off Surfside Beach in August, 1983, trying to decide if she were going to pay us a visit, I went to our monthly deacons' meeting. Three deacons out of 40 showed up. I went home and said to Alice and our three daughters, 'Let's pack the car; we're leaving tonight.'" Brother Joe said, "Pastor, I believe I understand what you're saying. It's every man for himself."

I counted Joe Brumbelow a dear friend and colleague in ministry. We prayed together. We cried together. We served together. I was guided by his wise counsel and encouraged by his godly example. He always preferred others above himself. When he became part of our staff in the role of minister of pastoral care, he lifted a heavy burden from me. I said, "Brother Joe, you will become the most beloved member of our staff." My words proved true.

For three years he conducted our Wednesday-night prayer service. He loved to preach; I deeply appreciated his help. Our folks thoroughly enjoyed his sermons and his humor. He always had a fresh, funny story to tell and an encouraging and uplifting word to share. He always began the service by inviting the people to pray for their pastor.

My association with the Brumbelow family continues to this day. I am honored to serve as Bonnie's pastor. Steve, their evangelist son, recently preached a successful crusade for us. David, their pastor son, serves a church in Highlands, Texas. Mark, their deacon son, lives nearby in Wild Peach. The Brumbelows are much-loved by the Hatches. No family exhibits more of the fruit of the Spirit or more of the character qualities of Christ than does the Brumbelow family.

I was privileged to preach Brother Joe's memorial service at First Baptist Church of Lake Jackson, after his three sons had paid tribute to their dad. A wonderful group of pastor friends, longtime acquaintances, and fellow church members gathered to give tribute to his memory. It was a great time of celebration.

Brother Joe, we salute you! You remain alive in our hearts. We look forward to a glad day of reunion. Thanks a million for all you did to bless our lives. And thank you, David Brumbelow, for sharing your father with us.

Dr. John A. Hatch, Pastor
First Baptist Church, Lake Jackson, TX
fbclj.org

(Dr. John A. Hatch has served as pastor in both Texas and Washington State. He is a graduate of East Texas Baptist University and Southwestern Baptist Theological Seminary. Among other positions, he has served as trustee of the International Mission Board and of East Texas Baptist University.)

Introduction

This book is intended to be an informal look at the wit and wisdom of my dad, Joseph Eldredge Brumbelow (pronounced Brum´-below), a longtime Texas pastor. The stories contained are gleaned from Joe Brumbelow's lifetime in the gospel ministry. Originality is not claimed for all the stories and quips. Preachers are notorious for borrowing illustrations and jokes from each other. The personal stories and references, however, are truthful. Joe used to say that he should write a book about his experiences in the ministry, but if he did, no one would believe it. I have checked the personal references and also have checked them with Mom and my two brothers. To the best of our memory, we have tried to be accurate.

This book is in no particular order—just personal memories I have of him. It is a little of everything—personal stories, sermon illustrations, poems, sayings, and jokes he enjoyed. Hunting and fishing stories, gardening information, history, folklore, and the perspective of a pastor's wife also are here. It contains the spiritual, the secular, and the in-between. But then, God's world includes them all.

Joe E. Brumbelow never was pastor of a large, prestigious church. He never was famous, wealthy, or powerful. He never held high office in his denomination.

He was, however, a remarkable person. He positively influenced both the well-known and the unknown. He believed that every word of the Bible is the inspired, inerrant Word of God. He had an outstanding love for his church and for those who did not know Christ as their Savior. Joe loved humor and used it in his preaching. He loved his family.

I could go on, but as he once said when introducing his son, Steve, to preach: "If he is as good as we say he is, we shouldn't put it off any longer. And if he's not, we need to get it over with!"

May this book be used to glorify God. May it bring a little knowledge and humor to those who know the Lord and love His appearing (2 Tim. 4:8 KJV).

David R. Brumbelow
Highlands, TX
May 1, 2005

(When this book refers to a preacher or others, certainly I'm not attempting to give an overall picture of that person's life and ministry. Just because I refer to only one humorous incident in the life of a preacher, I in no way am trying to minimize his ministry. See "Laughing at Ourselves and Others" in Chapter 2.)

Chapter 1

The Sin unto Death

Brother Joe preached about God's deadlines. God is a God of love, but He also is holy and a God of judgment. God's deadlines include sinning away your day of grace (Gen. 6:3), the unpardonable sin (Matt. 12:22-32), and the sin unto death.

Joe believed the first two deadlines were crossed only by someone who never had been saved. But a saved person could commit the sin unto death. Scripture says in 1 John 5:16, "There is a sin leading to death." To illustrate the biblical truth that a Christian, eternally secure, could commit the sin unto death, Brother Joe would use the following personal story:

"When I was a boy growing up in Damon, Texas, I would play in the front yard with my friends. Before long, we would disagree about something. We would start fussing and fighting. My mother would open the screen door and get on to me. I would promise to behave, but it would happen again. This time mother would tell me, 'Joe, your father has a good name in this community. You're hurting his name by acting this way. This is your last chance. If you don't straighten up, you will have to come inside and can't play with your friends any more.'

"'I'll stop fussing and fighting. I promise,' I would say. You guessed it. It happened again. My mother said, 'Joe, that was your last chance. Come inside right now.' No matter how much I protested, begged, and pleaded, I could not play with my friends any more that day. I was sent inside.

"Sometimes God says to His child, 'You're hurting My good name. Your influence is driving people away from Me. I've given you your last chance. Now I'm going to bring you home.'"

Staying Close to Jesus

Joe never knew why his dad sent him to school one year early. His sister, Myrtle Montier, since has explained. His dad was 49 when Joe was born. He was concerned that he might not live long enough to see his children graduate from school. He paid for them to start early.

Joe ended up being one of the smallest boys in his class at Damon. A bully began to go after him. Someone told Joe that a bully is just a lot of hot air and bluff. If you stand up to him, he will get scared and run. You won't have any more trouble out of him. Joe later would say, "That was some of the worst advice I ever had!" He tried it; the bully whipped him.

Sometime later the bully began picking on Johnny. One day Johnny had enough and whipped the bully. Joe then made friends with Johnny. "As long as I stayed around Johnny," said Joe, "I never had to worry about the bully bothering me."

If you try to whip the devil on your own, Joe explained, he will beat you every time. But Jesus defeated Satan at Calvary. Stay close to Jesus; you can whip the devil every time.

Little Boy Kicking Girl at Doverside.

Joe served as pastor of Doverside Baptist Church on the north side of Houston (619 Berry Rd., Houston, TX) from 1955 to 1963 and then was called back to serve as pastor there from 1970 to 1976. Doverside later merged with North Side Baptist on Bauman Road in Houston. North Side called him as pastor in 1987. Essentially, he was pastor of the same church three different times. Some would say to Joe, "They must really like you." He would reply, "They're just trying to give me another chance to get it right."

When he went back to Doverside in 1970, the community had gone through quite a transformation. Despite some strong opposition from a minority in the church, Joe believed in reaching and welcoming all people in the community. He began preparing the church for that. When Joe won a black teen-ager to the Lord, he baptized that teen like he would anyone else. A family left the church over it. The rest of the church members continued to support the church and pastor.

Joe realized that many in the community felt uncomfortable attending a predominately white church. A low-rent, government housing apartment project now bordered the church property on two sides. Doverside members wanted the residents to feel more welcomed to the church. The apartment dwellers walked across the back of the church property to get to stores a block or so away. The apartment management told the church it could block off access so the people could not cross church property. Instead, members of Doverside welcomed them and even laid a concrete sidewalk across the back of their property so the residents did not have to walk through the mud in rainy weather.

Then, members of Doverside started a Bible club. They began the club in the pastor's back yard that was at the back of the church property. Later they moved into the Fellowship Hall. Most of the children from the apartments were from broken homes. Some had real behavioral problems. Discipline often was necessary. Sometimes a child or two had to be sent home.

One day, as the kids waited in line to go inside, Joe saw a little boy go over to a little girl and kick her in the leg so hard she fell to the ground in tears. Joe grabbed the little boy and gave him a talking to. He spoke to him so sternly, the boy began to cry. Joe, seeing his tears, then gave him a big hug. He told him that he loved him, but he could not allow that kind of behavior.

Another little fellow saw the first boy kick the girl. He saw the preacher grab him, shake him, and rebuke him. Then he saw the preacher give the boy a big hug and tell him that he loved him. "So help me," Brother Joe said, "that second little fellow went over and kicked the same girl. That second boy was saying, 'I want to be loved, too. I want somebody to hug me, too.' The preacher then went through the same routine with the second boy. Joe said, "It was difficult on the little girl, but I got the message. Everyone out there needs someone to love them."

16

Tithe and Salary at Clegg

While in college at the University of Corpus Christi (UCC), Joe worked full time at Cagle's Service Station at the corner of Weber and Alameda streets in Corpus Christi (For the information of young folks, a service station is a full-service gas station. Employees check your tires and oil, wash your windows, do mechanic work, etc.). At the same time he also was pastor of the Baptist church at the little community of Clegg, TX. Clegg was a ranching community that was then in the fifth year of a seven-year drought. Their pastor's salary was half the church's Sunday offering. Joe would give a tithe (10 percent) of his service-station salary to the church where he was pastor. His tithe was about $7 each week; that would be about what his church salary turned out to be each week.

The exception was on the fifth Sunday. Then the church sent to a children's ministry what would have been his salary.

Learn from Preachers, but Don't Imitate Them

When Joe was a young preacher, one of the leading preachers of the day was R. G. Lee, pastor of the Bellevue Baptist Church, Memphis, TN. Joe decided he was going to try to preach like him. He heard Lester Roloff, then pastor of Second Baptist Church, Corpus Christi, and wondered whether to try to preach like him. Then he went to hear B. B. Crimm, a colorful, old-fashioned country evangelist. Crimm joked, kidded, and put on a show for the first 30 or 45 minutes of the service. Then he got serious about preaching. Crimm preached a great message from the Word of God; people trusted Christ as Savior.

Joe said he learned a lesson that day. God greatly used B. B. Crimm; he did not preach like anyone else. If God could use Crimm just the way he was, Joe decided God could use him just the way he was. Joe started preaching like no one else—the way God had called him and equipped him to preach. He decided to learn from others but not to imitate them.

Stomach Problems

When in college and early in his ministry Joe occasionally had a real problem with ulcers. No remedies seemed to do much good. He heard Lester Roloff praising the virtues of citrus. Joe remembered him saying something to the effect that if you have health and stomach problems, eat and drink more citrus. Joe decided that was the thing to do. He stopped eating much of anything else and started buying oranges. In retrospect, he said that was about the worst thing he could have done for his stomach problems. The overload of acid from the citrus just about killed him! After he recovered, he said from then on if he wanted to hear good preaching he would go hear Roloff; if he needed medical advice, he would see his doctor.

Borrowing Sermons and Illustrations

Preachers are known to borrow sermon outlines, sermons, and illustrations from others. Brother Joe quipped that if you use one source for your sermon, that's plagiarism. If you use two sources for your sermon, that's research!

He also told of the young preacher who was determined he would be original or nothing. He turned out to be both!

Suppose My Son Would Say to Me . . .

In the early 1970s Dad and I attended the Texas Evangelism Conference. One of the preachers was Dr. Roy Fish, evangelism professor at Southwestern Baptist Theological Seminary. In his sermon Dr. Fish used an outstanding illustration concerning being afraid to surrender to the will of God.

Dr. Fish said something like this: "Suppose when I get home, my son would come to me and say, 'Dad, I love you and want to be an obedient son. I want you to be proud of me. I want to start doing everything you want me to do.' Do you think I would make him do everything he hated and make his life miserable? Of course not. I would be so proud that he loved me and wanted to obey me that I would probably take him out to get an ice-cream cone. On the way back I might stop and buy him that baseball glove he's been wanting. That is how God feels about us. Don't be afraid of His will. God is a much better father than we will ever be."

We were impressed with that illustration. The following Sunday, Dad did not preach Fish's sermon, but he did use that illustration in his message. The next night Dad took the youth in his church to a Houston-area evangelism rally. Dr. Fish was preaching. Dad said to me, "You don't think there's any chance he will preach the same sermon or use that same illustration?" "No," I said, "I doubt it."

In the middle of his message, however, Fish began, "Suppose my boy were to say to me . . ." Lydia Tamez, the girl sitting next to me, whispered, "That sounds familiar." Dad was sitting in the row in front of me. I saw him sliding down in his seat!

The story does not end there. A year or two later, I was reading the book, *The Holy Spirit: Who He Is and What He Does,* by R. A. Torrey. It was copyrighted in 1927 by the Fleming H. Revell Company. On page 170 Torrey said, "Suppose when I get back to Chicago, my son . . ." The same illustration! I am confident that if I had access to earlier sermon books, I could find where Torrey also "borrowed" that illustration.

So no one misunderstands: Sometimes, like the above story, a preacher can adapt the illustration to himself or think of a similar personal incident that he can use to illustrate the same point. But Dad never told someone else's story as though it happened to him (unless he clearly was joking). That's just plain lying.

The story is told of one preacher who did steal other people's exploits. The congregation added up how old he must be if he had done everything he said he had done. Members concluded he must be about 120 years old!

Balance in Your Ministry
Joe lived through many fads and was known for his balance. He preached the whole Word of God and stood for its truth and

divine inspiration. At times he saw the Christian bookstore shelves filled with books on angels. Other times they filled with books about demons and Satan. He saw some preachers who wanted only to preach about prophecy, or demon possession, or the deeper life. Brother Joe believed you couldn't get any deeper than leading someone to Jesus. Some wanted only the flashiest preachers and the biggest circus acts. Joe preached on all the above topics. He was staunchly premillennial. But he never went to seed (overemphasized one doctrine and diminished or excluded others—a farming term about letting crops grow too long before they are harvested. A crop such as greens will form a seed head and turn bitter) on any of these teachings.

Public Confession
One fad that occasionally raises its head is the idea that a believer should tell to the class or the entire church every bad thing he or she ever has done. This has caused much needless shame and many awkward situations. Joe knew about an incident when a man stood in a church and, pointing out another man's wife, confessed he had been having lustful thoughts about her. That only made things uncomfortable for her (an innocent party), her husband, and everyone present.

We are to confess all our sins to God, but we do not always need to air our dirty laundry in public. Joe believed a good general rule to follow is that public sins were to be confessed publicly and private sins were to be confessed privately. Of course some private sins can become public and have far-reaching consequences. At times a detailed confession needs to be made to the church, but not always. Sometimes a person may need to make a general confession to the church. Some in the church may know the details, but all the details do not always need to be shared.

How wonderful, however, that God knows every bad thing about us and still loves us! God will forgive and cleanse us if we confess to Him our sin (1 John 1:7-9; Ps. 32; 51).

I'm the Little Boy With the Candy

Joe Brumbelow used the following illustration: Years ago a poor, ragged boy pressed his face against the window of a candy store. Clearly he had no money and only could look. A businessman saw the boy and the candy store. "Would you like some candy?" the man asked the boy. "You bet I would, Mister," the boy replied. "Let's go in; I'll buy you a dime's worth of candy." That was in the days when a dime bought a lot of candy. The clerk got a sack and began getting a piece of this candy and that, as the boy excitedly pointed them out.

The businessman paid for the candy. The little boy took his sack and gleefully went outside, sat down on the curb, and began eating his candy. The man watched him for a while and then asked, "Is the candy good?" "Yes, sir," was the reply. "Son, could I have a piece of that candy?" the man asked. Suddenly the boy grasped the sack tightly to himself, jumped up and said, "It's my candy." He ran down the street hollering, "It's mine. It's mine. It's mine."

God gives us life and all that we have. Then He asks us to give 10 percent—the tithe—to Him. Much like the little boy, we reply, "It's mine. It's mine. It's mine."

When he preached a revival, Joe often preached on the subject of tithing. He was surprised how many people were saved when he preached on this subject that seemed to be just for believers. During a revival in Kingsville he preached on tithing and used the above illustration. Back home at Cypress Brother Joe received the following letter from a man in Kingsville: "Sir, just thought you'd like to know: I'm the little boy that ran off with the sack. And sir, also thought you'd like to know: I came back and said, 'Please, kind sir, forgive my greedy heart and please, sir, take not one piece, but take the whole sack.'" Signed, _____. (Letter dated April 15, 1970)

Dramatic Testimonies

Reading the testimony of the Apostle Paul (Acts 9, 22) is thrilling. Many today have such dramatic testimonies. Joe believed in the power of testimonies to reach the lost. He had Dan Vestal and Allan Buchanek preach and give their outstanding testimonies. He even had a testimony revival. A different speaker each night of the week gave a testimony of how he or she found Christ as Savior.

Joe was aware, however, of three things: First, he knew that the greatest testimony is that of a Daniel or a Joseph who grew up serving the Lord and never strayed away. (The problem is that giving that kind of testimony without it being boring or sounding prideful is difficult.)

Second, he knew to be careful of the novice. A new Christian, no matter how high-profile, should be given a year or two to get his or her spiritual feet on the ground. Once that person has been grounded in the Christian life and the Bible, then that individual can begin sharing his testimony.

Third, he knew to beware of the charlatan. Many have scheduled a dramatic preacher to speak and later found out he was a fraud. Check him out.

Any believer, however, can personally share a testimony. Simply tell what your life was like before you knew Jesus, how you met Jesus as your Savior, and what your life has been like since meeting Jesus. This is one of the most effective ways of witnessing. Your testimony does not have to be exciting or dramatic. Most aren't, but they always tell about the amazing love and grace of God for the sinner needing forgiveness.

Divine Healing

Joe believed in faith-healing but not faith-healers. He believed that God heals; sometimes He chooses to heal miraculously, but not always. He recalled the time a friend told him about delivering numerous prescription drugs to a well-known, Houston faith-healer. Why did a faith-healer need those drugs?

He also wondered why he knew of no 100-year-old faith-healers. He noted, "They get sick and die, just like Baptist preachers do."

It Was Good for Paul and Silas

Brother Joe grew up reading, loving, and preferring the King James Version of the English Bible. But he did not fall in with the King-James-Only crowd. He believed the historic Christian doctrine of the inspiration and inerrancy of the Bible in the original manuscripts, not in a particular English translation. He would joke about those who seem to believe, "If the King James Version was good enough for the Apostle Paul, it's good enough for me."

He also thought it was ironic that those who make the most of the 1611 KJV apparently did not realize that they were not using the 1611 KJV. The old KJV that people use today actually was revised several times after 1611.

On the radio Joe once heard a proponent of KJV-Only preaching about a ministry in Israel. The preacher said he was providing Bibles to the people. He wanted the radio listeners to know what kind of Bibles and assured, "They are Hebrew Bibles in the King James Version."

(For those new to the Bible, the Old Testament originally was written in Hebrew and the New Testament in Greek. If you do not know Greek or Hebrew, you'll be thankful for the good English translations of the Bible we have available today. Joe was familiar with other good English translations such as the New King James Version, New American Standard Bible, and the New International Version. For more information, see Appendix 1.)

The Vet

Brother Joe visited one of his church members in Houston. The husband was sick, but his wife could not get him to go to the doctor. The pastor kidded, "If you won't go to the doctor, we may just have to take you to the veterinarian!" The man's wife replied, "But Brother Joe, he isn't a veteran."

God's Missing

Joe told the story of two little boys with real behavior problems. Their mother could not straighten them up. She decided to let the preacher do the job. She dropped them off at the preacher's office. One sat in the outer office while the oldest entered it. The preacher decided to teach them a little theology about the omnipresence of God. He looked at the boy and asked, "Where's God?" The boy sat in silence. "Where's God?", the preacher asked again. Silence. A little frustrated, the preacher said, "Son, I'm asking you a question. Where is God?" The boy jumped up and ran out of the office. As he ran by his little brother, he cried, "Let's get out of here. God's missing, and they think we did it!"

Child Discipline and the New Psychology

Joe believed in old-fashioned, loving discipline. He disagreed with some of the new ideas about letting children bloom on their own or decide for themselves whether they would attend church. To those who could not control their little children he told about a boy misbehaving in a grocery store. The mother told the manager, "I can't do anything with him." The manager said, "Let me try." He walked over and whispered something in the boy's ear. The little boy suddenly was transformed. He followed his mother around the store and did not cause any more trouble.

The astounded mother asked the store manager, "What in the world did you do? He's acting so much better. Was it some of the new psychology? "No," replied the manager. "I just told him if he didn't straighten up, I was going to beat the devil out of him."

What Shall It Profit a Preacher if He Wins the Whole World and Loses His Own Family?

Too many pastors give their all to their church and neglect their families. Like Eli and Samuel, some godly pastors are poor fathers. Joe was aware of one great preacher whose son returned home to die as a drunkard. The preacher later preached on the Scripture, "Other vineyards have I kept, but mine own vineyard have I not kept." Joe knew of another great preacher whose son was asked about his father after his father's death. The preacher's son replied, "I have nothing to say. I never really knew him."

Joe Brumbelow never wanted that to be true of him. Through the years he said, "I would rather it be said of me that I was a great husband and father than that I was a great preacher."

Urging a Church Member to Stay

One great lesson Joe learned after some years in the ministry was not to talk people out of leaving the church. Looking back on his early ministry, he was convinced that he had talked some people into staying in the church when they would have been better off leaving.

In his later ministry, if someone threatened to leave the church, he would let them. He sometimes would say, "I believe you know the Lord and that you are willing to follow His will. If you believe it is God's will for you to leave this church, I'm not going to try to talk you out of it." How could they expect the pastor to talk them out of doing God's will? That kind of attitude on his part seemed to solve some real problems.

Staying in the Ministry

When Joe surrendered to the ministry, an aunt told him, "You probably won't last. Not many do."

That may have turned out to be one of his best incentives. Times of discouragement occurred when, if for no other reason, he determined he was not going to leave the ministry and give that aunt the satisfaction of being right.

Preachers Considering Leaving the Ministry

Joe once heard of a survey showing something like 75 percent of pastors had considered leaving the ministry. The speaker at a pastor's meeting expressed his shock at the high percentage that had thought of leaving. Joe quipped, "I was shocked, too. I was shocked that the other 25 percent lied."

A pastor's ministry can be stressful. Much of the stress goes on behind the scenes unnoticed by most. Probably no pastor of more than six months has gone without a thought of leaving the ministry.

To Stay, or Not

Dad told me of the following exchange of two Houston Baptist pastors. One had been at his church for many years. The other was known for going to a new church every couple of years. The pastor not known for his longevity at any one church told his fellow pastor, "Why don't you let me give you a sermon so you can get a new church?" The other replied, "Why don't you let me give you a sermon so you can keep a church?"

Resigning as Pastor

Brother Joe believed in leaving a church on good terms. Many a pastor, when he is ready to resign, makes a mental list of all the slights the church has dealt him. Life is not fair; every pastor is mistreated in some way. But the church has called the pastor to help and not hurt it. Joe left on a positive note; it always did him and the church a world of good. He was loved by his former members and often was asked to return to former pastorates for Homecoming days.

Charismatics

Did you hear about the plane-load of charismatics? The flight attendant announced, "Anyone who wants a cup of coffee, please lower your hand."

Gluttony

Once Joe had been on a diet and had lost a good deal of weight. He naturally was gratified at his accomplishment. On losing the weight, he offered some friendly advice to one of his overweight preacher friends, "You know, gluttony is a sin." His friend replied, "I know, Joe; so is pride."

Getting Taken Advantage of

Joe served as pastor of churches in low-income areas and often dealt with those asking for assistance. It was one of his most stressful jobs. He tried to help the needy and turn down the con artists.

He knew that sometimes he got taken in. But he said, "I had rather be taken in from time to time than get so hard-hearted that no one could take advantage of me."

The Heifer

In one of his early pastorates the rumor went around that a man in Joe's church called a woman in the church an old heifer. Joe and another man from the church went to visit him and to try to quash the rumor. Joe said something like, "There's a rumor going around the church. You know how false stories can get started. I know you didn't really call Mrs. ___ an old heifer." "Yes, I did!" the man replied. "That's exactly what I said." Thus ended the young pastor's rumor-busting for the day.

Partial List of Men Joe Brumbelow Admired in the Ministry

• R. G. Lee; pastor of Bellevue Baptist Church, Memphis, TN. An old-time, eloquent preacher.

• Dan Vestal, Sr.; evangelist. Joe asked him to preach in numerous revivals. Preached his famous testimony, "Why the Scar on My Face."

• B. B. Crimm; he was a colorful, controversial, powerful evangelist.

• Lester Roloff; colorful, controversial preacher in Corpus Christi. Admirers would usually start by saying, "I don't agree with him on everything, but . . ." He was a great preacher of the Word. One of Joe's members at First Baptist Church, Dawson— Aldon Nesmith—was the first person that Roloff led to the Lord when Roloff began his ministry. Roloff grew up in the Dawson area and was pastor of Shiloh Baptist Church. When Joe was in

Dawson, the Shiloh church out in the country had disbanded. Most of the former members were at FBC, Dawson.

• John R. Rice; independent Baptist preacher and author. Joe did not agree with him on all matters but appreciated his conservative stand on the basic doctrines of the Christian faith, his soul-winning, his emphasis on great preachers and missionaries of the past, and his concern for the Christian home.

• Paige Patterson; now president of Southwestern Baptist Theological Seminary, Fort Worth, TX. A personal friend and a first-class scholar, although he does not act like one. Joe appreciated someone who was intelligent but did not have to act like he was. He admired Paige's stand and sacrifices for the benefit of the Southern Baptist Convention. He loved visiting with Paige and his wife, Dorothy, at the annual Southern Baptist Convention meeting.

• W. A. Criswell; author and longtime pastor of First Baptist Church, Dallas. Used his commentaries; especially liked the one on Revelation. Liked his preaching and his conservative stand.

• Judge Paul Pressler; committed Christian judge and leader in the conservative resurgence in the SBC. A personal friend, he and his wife, Nancy, were some of Joe's heroes.

• Adrian Rogers; pastor of Bellevue Baptist Church, Cordova, TN. Joe thought him probably the best living preacher in America. Admired his ability to speak the truth in love (Eph. 4:15).

• Harvey Graham; great old-time Texas Baptist preacher, singer, musician. Was Joe and Bonnie's pastor when they were in college at UCC. Great preacher of the gospel and could sing *Old-Fashioned Meeting* and *In Shady Green Pastures* like no one else. Played the piano and accordion. Had five daughters: four married preachers; the other married a deacon.

• Jerry Vines; great preacher, author, and pastor of First Baptist Church, Jacksonville, FL.

• B. H. Carroll; founder of Southwestern Seminary. Joe was impressed with his testimony, *My Infidelity and What Became of It*. When others were beginning to deny the inspiration of the

Bible, Carroll stood for the complete truthfulness and verbal inspiration of the Word of God.

• H. A. Ironside; pastor of Moody Memorial Church, Chicago, IL. Joe often used his commentaries; especially liked the one on 1 Corinthians.

• O. O. Ervin; a fellow student at UCC; pastor in Corpus Christi, Bynum, Kingsville, New London, and South Padre Island. Joe said, "I learned more about winning the lost to Jesus from Brother Ervin than from anyone else."

(I know the above is true. As previously noted, this is only a partial list; Joe would have included many others. Unfortunately, he is not around to ask about the others. Someone has said, "When a senior citizen dies, it is like a library burning down.")

Don't Let Your Daughter Date until She's 18
Joe had Harvey Graham preach a revival for him. They visited a man who was having trouble with his teen-age daughter. Harvey offered some of his counsel on raising children. Harvey had refused to let any of his five daughters date until they were 18 years old. During the visit he emphasized that to the father.

As they left the house, Harvey asked, "Joe, how old was Bonnie when you got married?" "Seventeen," Joe replied. Harvey said, "I thought you were being awfully quiet in there."

Maybe a Cigarette Now and Then
In the 1950s a revival was being held at Doverside. During the invitation one morning a visiting woman, whom no one seemed to know, said she wanted to speak. Against his better judgment the evangelist, Dan Vestal, allowed her to do so. She spoke of how she had received the "second blessing": attained a level in her spiritual life where she no longer sinned. She urged others to reach for this state of sinless perfection.

She became more animated. She wore a heavy coat. At one point her hand hit the side of her coat; a long cigarette flipped out of the pocket and fell in the center church aisle.

Evangelist Dan Vestal walked over and picked up the cigarette for all to see. The woman stuttered and stammered a little and allowed as how she may still have a fault or two. She was never seen at the church again.

Joe claimed he had the second blessing, and the third, and fourth, fifth, and the thousandth. But he knew the Bible and knew himself well enough to know he would not reach sinless perfection in this life (1 John 1:8).

First Lady and First Cook

As a preacher's wife Bonnie not only cooked for the family but also for numerous evangelists, church events, summer missionaries, family meals after funerals, and other occasions. I am not alone in saying she has excelled at the job of cooking.

Cooking and serving a meal can be a real ministry for a church or an individual. Mildred McWhorter of the Baptist Mission Centers in Houston told Bonnie, "When I heard your church was bringing the meal for the summer missionaries, I knew that it would be great." It was not just her cooking, but Joe and Bonnie led their church (First Baptist Church, Cypress, at that time) to send their best for the workers at the mission center. Some churches moan when they have to prepare a meal for others, but it can be one of their most meaningful ministries. Jesus taught that if you have done it for them in My name, you've done it unto Me. What a meal we'd prepare for Jesus! (Matt. 25:35-40; Mark 9:41)

(Bonnie Brumbelow has written a cookbook, *Masterpieces from Our Kitchen*. She has tried and proved every one of the 233 recipes from her 50 years experience as a pastor's wife. For more information see Appendix 1.)

Chapter 2

She's Awake Now

You never made the mistake twice of asking a certain preacher friend to bless the food in a restaurant. He prayed long and loud. He had a booming voice. The attention of the whole restaurant immediately would be brought to bear on the other embarrassed folks at the table. Joe, on the other hand, kept his mealtime prayers short and sweet. He joked that when you bless the meal, that's no time to pray for the missionaries.

On one occasion the preacher mentioned above attended a revival service. Afterward he was invited to our home for a meal with the evangelist, Dan Vestal, and our family. As usual, they visited, laughed, and joked into the night. For those who aren't preachers, you might understand that this behavior is one of their best therapies. Bonnie finally excused herself and disappeared into the bedroom. Sometime later as they were about to disperse, they asked this preacher to pray. Pray he did. After he prayed, he asked, "Is Bonnie asleep?" Vestal replied, "She's not now!"

The Baptism of Linda Potts

Joe ministered to a unique couple named Robert and Linda Potts. He was blind; she had no legs. He would push her wheelchair; she would give him directions. They had a wonderful sense of humor. Robert would say, "Let's go hear a movie."

Joe won them to the Lord; they became candidates for baptism. Baptism was a real victory for Linda. Besides, and perhaps because of her handicap, she had a great fear of water.

The question was, How do we baptize Linda? First, she had no legs. Second, she was full-figured. She knew that baptism was not necessary for salvation, but if at all possible, she wanted to be obedient to this command of our Lord. Baptists, of course, believe in believer's baptism by immersion.

Brother Joe chose two deacons to assist. They placed Linda in a metal lawn chair and carried her up the steps, then down the steps into the baptistry. They set her in the water. Joe began to try to lower her into the water. They expected the problem would be that she would sink, so they were ready to hold her up; instead she floated like a cork. Joe tried to ease her under the water. Then he tried again, still without success. When part of her went under, another part popped up. At one point in frustration he placed his hand on her stomach and tried to shove her down. She involuntarily let out a loud, "Whooo."

Joe later said, "I may not have gotten her under all at once, but I did get her all wet."

Why Believer's Baptism by Immersion?

To Brother Joe his final, infallible source was the Bible. He explained the following:

The New Testament Greek word for *baptize* means "to immerse, dip, or plunge."

Baptism is a symbol of a death, burial, and resurrection. When you bury someone, you don't throw a little dirt on his face and say he is buried. You cover him with dirt.

In the Bible, faith in Christ always occurs first, then baptism. That is why we do not baptize babies but insist that a child be old enough to personally accept Jesus as his or her Savior.

Salvation is dying to our old life of sin and being resurrected to a new life in Jesus. Baptism is a symbol—a picture of what happens when a person is saved (born again). Being baptized before you are saved is like having your funeral before you die.

Baptism symbolizes three things: death, burial, and resurrection.

The person being baptized is showing his or her belief in the following:

32

First, I believe Jesus died for my sins, was buried, and rose again.

Second, I have died to my old life of sin and have been raised to walk in newness of life in Jesus.

Third, when the Christian dies physically, his body is laid in the grave and his spirit goes to be with the Lord. But when Jesus returns, He will bring with Him those (the souls, spirits) who sleep in Jesus. Their physical bodies then will be raised from the grave (1 Thess. 4:13-18).

When you are baptized, you are preaching a sermon to the world without having to say a word. You are saying you believe in the above truths about baptism (Matt. 28:19; Mark 1:9; Rom. 6:4; Col. 2:12-13).

Baptism is the first command of God to the new Christian, but it does not save. Only personal faith in Jesus as Lord and Savior saves (Eph. 2:8-9).

A Hill on Which to Die

"Joe Brumbelow was a pastor at First Baptist Church of Dawson, Texas, near Corsicana, when we first met. Now he is on the staff of First Baptist Church of Lake Jackson, Texas. He and his wife, Bonnie, are the parents of three sons, two of whom also have served as Southern Baptist pastors. Steve built a fine work in West Virginia, where building churches is difficult. We served together on the Executive Committee (of the Southern Baptist Convention). Now he is an evangelist. The second son, David, now pastors effectively in Highlands, near Houston. Their other son, Mark, is in business and is a deacon and Sunday School teacher in a Southern Baptist church.

"They represent what a Christian family should be. They love the Lord, serve Him faithfully, and have unselfishly given of themselves. They and others like them are the heart and soul of the conservative movement."—Judge Paul Pressler, *A Hill On Which To Die*, Broadman & Holman Publishers; 1999. From the chapter, "My Heroes of the Resurgence".

The Battle for the Bible

Joe Brumbelow was proud to have been involved in the conservative resurgence in the Southern Baptist Convention (SBC). He and Bonnie attended each year's convention, though for them to do so was a financial sacrifice. At the height of the controversy, we would be at the convention center before the doors opened Tuesday morning so we could get a seat. Bonnie at times smuggled food into the convention center so we could keep our seats until the presidential election and other business of the afternoon was over. Like many a dutiful pastor's wife, she often kept our seats while the preachers in the family went out in the hallways to fellowship and catch up on the latest jokes, politics, etc.

To Brother Joe this controversy was not just a fight among preachers. It was a very spiritual issue. He believed that if the SBC turned from its commitment to the truthfulness of Scripture, we also would lose the zeal to win people to the Lord. If we don't believe in hell, we do not have much need for a Savior. Joe prayed often about the issue and was thrilled that the SBC, our seminaries, and our mission boards were turned back to our historic doctrines. These institutions now are led by those who believe in the inerrancy of the Bible. Before he went to be with the Lord, he saw the accuracy of his predictions by seeing the conservative-led SBC continue to start churches, win many to the Lord, and grow in numbers. He saw those leaving the SBC decline in numbers and de-emphasize soul winning, thereby winning few and starting few new churches. To him it wasn't a power struggle; it was a struggle over doctrine and over the eternal destiny of lost souls.

Joe knew that conservatives were not perfect, but he believed they were right on the major issues. He had good friends who were on the moderate side. He loved to fellowship, laugh, and joke with them. He knew that they knew and loved the Lord. But he sincerely believed that they were wrong. Brother Joe believed that if the SBC allowed belief in the inerrancy of Scripture to become optional for our seminary professors and missionaries, it would begin a slow decline in evangelism, missions, and the great doctrines of our faith.

(Joe was impressed with several books on the history of the SBC conservative resurgence. Those books included those written by James Hefley, Paul Pressler, and Jerry Sutton. He was referred to in one way or another in more than one of Hefley's *Truth in Crisis* books as well as Pressler's book. See Appendix 1.)

The Weeping Prophet

To many of his peers Joe Brumbelow was known as the Weeping Prophet because of his tears in his preaching and his tears for the lost. Pastor Ed Weatherly recently told me he had Joe preach years before at what used to be called a Premillennial Bible Conference. Joe preached on the Tribulation. Pastor Weatherly said it was the best sermon he had ever heard on that subject. He said he remembered Joe's tears as he preached. Brother Joe really believed the biblical truth that the lost are headed to hell and that their only hope is Jesus.

I remember accepting Jesus as my Savior at the young age of 5. I did not know all about the Bible, but even at that age I knew that I was a sinner and that Jesus loved me and died for me. One Sunday at the conclusion of the worship service, during the invitation (a time when people are asked to publicly respond to the message by going forward for prayer or to make a decision for Christ), I went forward, took Dad by the hand, and told him I wanted to be saved. I still remember us kneeling before God that day. We prayed together; I asked Jesus to forgive my sins and enter my heart and be my Savior. I still remember, as our heads were together in prayer, feeling Dad's hot tears as they ran down his face and touched mine.

At his funeral, the organist, Dorothy Salser, told me she remembered that day, some 40 years earlier.

That was not an unusual event. Brother Joe never got over his tears and his love for the lost in need of a Savior.

Joe, We Better Get Out of Here!

Joe had Harvey Graham preach a revival. They visited a poor family in little more than a shack that was not very clean. As they sat in the living room, a baby in a diaper entered from another room. The diaper obviously was full. Every so often the baby would fall back on his bottom, then get up, and take another step or two. When he would get up, he would leave a puddle behind. To make matters worse, then the dog entered and began to lap the puddle. That was more than Harvey could take. Almost gagging he said, "Joe don't you think it's about time to leave? Joe, we better get out of here."

The Preacher and Personal Morality

No hint of immorality ever existed in Brother Joe's personal life and ministry. He was absolutely committed to his wife and family. He believed that preachers were to be especially careful in this area. He humorously told preachers to only shake a woman's hand and not for long, at that. He did not go around hugging all the women in the church. During the invitation he was careful in his physical contact and appearance with girls and women. As he received them at the front of the sanctuary, he had a way of holding his Bible up to a woman's shoulder with his left hand as he shook her hand with his right. He wanted to avoid even the appearance of evil. He did not travel or spend time alone with someone of the opposite gender. When he counseled someone of the opposite gender, he left his office door open.

A couple of humorous incidents, however, might be appropriate here:

At a Baptist meeting in another city he had checked into a motel and with key in hand (before the electronic key cards) went to his room. He opened the door, stepped in, and saw a woman sitting on the bed (fully clothed). In shock he said, "Oh, oh, oh." The motel had given him the wrong room. The woman happened to be a member of his previous church. She and her husband were attending the same conference as was Joe.

Once Joe returned home in the middle of the day in Corpus Christi and told Bonnie he wanted her to hear something before anyone else did. As he had been driving down Leopard Drive, one of the women in his church was on the side of the road. Her car had broken down; they saw each other, and he could do nothing else but offer her a ride. He was glad to help but wanted his wife to know before any rumors could get started.

Joe noted that sometimes a woman says she is attracted to a particular preacher because he is such a good, spiritual man. But if he is willing to commit adultery, he's not a good man.

People naturally are attracted to certain other people. But when someone of the opposite gender is attracted to a married preacher, while nothing may be wrong with that attraction so far, the attraction itself certainly should be a danger signal. Bonnie once told Joe about a woman in the church that had her eye on him. He joked with Bonnie about it, but he took her seriously and was doubly careful.

Joe knew a woman can see things that a man may not observe. Someone has said a man is a fool if he won't listen to his wife about such matters.

Loving the Unlovely

One of the first revivals evangelist James Robison preached was for Joe Brumbelow in Houston in the early 1960s. During that week Joe took the young Robison to a number of low-income homes, where they witnessed to the families. Afterward James sometimes talked about the most influential people in his life and named Brother Joe. James said, "Joe Brumbelow taught me how to love the unlovely."

That same week evangelist singer and preacher Billy Foote led the singing. Years later he wrote:

"To God be the glory for the memory of Joe Brumbelow, who died Aug. 30.

"Years ago, he returned a second time to pastor Doverside Baptist Church in Houston, which by then was in a low-income neighborhood. 'Bro. Joe, what made you feel led to go back to Doverside?' I asked him.

"'Oh, I kind of missed going into some of those little dirty houses, sitting in an old dirty couch, drinking out of an old dirty coffee cup, and having little dirty kids come up and get in my lap,' he said. 'Those little kids need Jesus. I just went back to where my heart was.'

"Most people never will know the Joe Brumbelows of this life, but it is the Joe Brumbelows and their kind who will receive the greatest reward in heaven, simply because they went about doing good, serving Jesus in the place where God put them with a pure heart." (Letter from Evangelist Billy Foote, Longview, TX, printed in the *Baptist Standard*, Dallas, TX; Sept. 23, 2002. Joe's obituary was in the *Baptist Standard* on Sept. 9, 2002.)

I Am the Preacher
On one occasion Joe was fishing on the seawall in Corpus Christi. He had an impressive stringer of speckled trout when other fishermen were not doing nearly so well. A passing tourist admired his catch and said, "You must be paying the preacher," to which Joe replied, "I am the preacher."

Alaska
In the 1970s Brother Joe preached a revival in Anderson, Alaska, near the Clear Air Force Base. It was a simultaneous revival effort through the Home Mission Board (now North American Mission Board). At an orientation meeting personnel learned that the work in Alaska often was difficult and warned participants not to expect a lot of visible results. On top of that, he found that the church in which he was to preach had military officials, doctors, and highly educated members. If that were not enough, the pastor, Jim Clark, was a member of MENSA, composed of those in the top five-percent IQ range.

Joe was convinced that revival would not occur those two weeks in Alaska. He prayed for revival, however, and preached

38

the biblical sermons he always had preached. He suspected that many attended just to hear his Southern accent. They enjoyed hearing him pronounce words such as *hell* and *pulpit*.

They told Joe that people were rugged individualists in Alaska and dressed as they pleased. They suggested that the preachers not necessarily wear coats and ties. Joe did not fault preachers when the popular thing later was not to wear a necktie. He recalled how John the Baptist had dressed (Mark 1:6) and that Jesus said, "There has not risen one greater than John the Baptist" (Matt. 11:11). But Joe was most comfortable preaching in a coat and tie. He decided, "If they are going to be individualists and dress as they please, I'll do the same." Joe wore a coat and tie throughout the revival. The Alaskans seemed to admire the fact that he also dressed as he pleased.

Despite Joe's dire concerns, a great revival occurred. God can work in Alaska just like He does in Texas or elsewhere. Sixteen people were saved. Joe and Jim Clark became lifelong friends.

This brings to mind one of Joe's stories about the young preacher who wrote home to his preacher dad about a problem. The son had just been called to a church in a university town. He told his dad that every time he preached and started to say something about science, he remembered that a scientist was in the congregation. When he spoke about history, he remembered that a history professor was present. He also was intimidated because of the English professor and the mathematician. "Dad, what am I supposed to do?" he asked. His father wrote back and said, "Son, just preach the Bible. They won't know a thing about it."

Aurora Borealis

Joe prized the beauty of nature. A trip was always more exciting when he saw wildlife. Stopping on the roadside or making a u-turn to see wildlife such as deer, geese, or sand-hill cranes was not uncommon.

In Alaska he saw moose, other wildlife, and numerous snow-capped mountains. Joe also saw what locals said was one of the best displays of the Aurora Borealis (northern lights) in years. Joe was sure his heavenly Father put on the display just for him. He was outside the house in Alaska when he saw the Aurora Borealis in all its glory. He would not go inside to tell the others lest it be gone when he returned. He didn't want to miss a moment of it, so he stayed outside and just beat on the side of the house until the others emerged.

Moral Crusade

Joe wade-fished at the Ship Channel in Corpus Christi which had some open, somewhat isolated land. Occasionally he saw a couple use the area as a place to rendezvous for immoral purposes. On cleaning his fish, he started throwing the scraps in the brush by the couple's meeting place. After a few days the smell was awful. He never saw the couple there again.

Gratitude

As a college student at University of Corpus Christi Joe heard through the grapevine about how the college president had made a real sacrifice in leaving the business world to serve as president of the small Baptist school.

One day on campus he approached President W.A. Miller and told him he had heard of that sacrifice and wanted to thank him for being at UCC (University of Corpus Christi). He thought that many others had said the same thing to him and that he would just be wasting the president's time. Joe was surprised, however, when President Miller paused, looked at him with moistened eyes, and said, "Thank you, son. No one has ever told me that before." It was a lesson in needing to express gratitude more often.

Looking toward Heaven

After Joe began his Doverside pastorate in 1955, he noticed something peculiar about the baptistry. Above the glass and window, looking out to the sanctuary, these words were on the wall:

"In obedience to the command of our Lord and Savior Jesus Christ, and upon your profession of faith, I baptize you, in the name of the Father, the Son, and the Holy Spirit."

He questioned the interim pastor, Brother Pepper, who confessed that he never could remember those words. When Brother Pepper baptized someone, he raised his hand, looked toward heaven, and read the words off the wall. He must have looked very spiritual doing so!

Is God Calling Me to the Ministry?

Advice Joe gave both his sons who talked to him at different times about whether God was calling them to surrender to the ministry: "If you can be happy doing anything else, do it." He loved the ministry and was not trying to keep us from following that call. His reasoning was that if God is really calling you to preach, you will not be happy doing anything else.

Bill Morgan

Joe had been concerned through the years that often when a preacher friend died, by the time he found out about it, the funeral had already taken place. (Perhaps our state papers can help in this with an Internet obituary page for ministers.) When Joe died suddenly and unexpectedly, in the midst of our shock and grief we tried to notify everyone we could. One close, old preacher friend of his was Bill Morgan. Bill had been pastor in Jersey Village and Alto. We tried but could not locate him.

The week after Dad's funeral we saw that Bill Morgan was listed in the obituaries in the *Baptist Standard*. He had died two or three weeks before Joe did. Had Joe known, he would have been at Bill Morgan's funeral. His wife contacted Mom not long after. I could not help thinking how surprised Joe was as he walked the streets of gold to see his good friend, Bill, already there.

Loving and Supporting All Your Kids

Joe and Bonnie had three sons. Two were called to preach; the other was not. At times someone would say, "You sure must be proud of your two preacher boys." Bonnie would reply, "I'm proud of all three of my boys."

Mark is the youngest of their three sons. He is a deacon, Sunday-school teacher, taxidermist, carpenter, and a fellow who can do just about anything for anybody. He and Cherry have reared an outstanding Christian family of three boys. Mom and Dad were just as proud of them as they were of any of us boys.

They loved us the same, but when we were children, they didn't treat us the same. They knew each child has different needs and that one type of discipline works better for some than for others. In other words, they knew just the kind of discipline for each of us that would hurt the worst!

Taking Care of Missions and Pastors

God provides, but He often chooses to do so through His church. Joe was of the old school, so he was very uncomfortable in talking to his church about his salary. He served as pastor of relatively small- to medium-sized churches whose members were not high-income. Like most other pastors, he never made a large salary.

A pastor has to pay bills and desires to take care of his family financially just like everyone else. Sometimes all that's required is a member asking the church (or asking the pastor) when was the last time our staff had a raise or even a cost-of-living adjustment. The local Baptist association or a banker can give you the cost-of-living (also called consumer price index or inflation-rate) percentages for the last several years. As churches, do all you reasonably can to take care of your pastor and staff. At least don't allow their salaries to decrease year after year through inflation.

He did not tell his church this, lest it look self-serving, but he mentioned it to others. Joe Brumbelow said, "In all my years of ministry I have never seen a church suffer from increasing giving to missions or from increasing the pastor's salary."

Some say a preacher is to live on faith. One of Joe's preacher friends said, "When I go to pay my bills, they don't want faith; they want cold, hard cash." (See Gal. 6:6; 1 Cor. 9:7-15; 1 Tim. 5:17-18; Prov. 27:18; Deut. 25:4.)

Laughing at Ourselves and Others
Joe had a great sense of humor and often laughed at himself and others. He received almost as much enjoyment out of a joke played on himself as those played on others. We three boys often joked with and played tricks on Dad, but he knew we also were doing it while still having a great amount of respect for him. He laughed about the time he referred in a sermon to the four-letter word *cross* and how in an illustration he badly mispronounced the name Napoleon Bonaparte.

He also made fun of other preachers while at the same time having great respect for them. Some of the stories in this book may lead some to think he had a condescending view of other preachers—especially some that are joked about in this book. That would not be correct. Joe loved jokes about preachers and could laugh at himself as well as at other preachers. He knew that preachers were not perfect. He knew that a preacher could have some weaknesses and peculiarities and still be greatly used of God. So when Joe respectfully made fun of preachers and others, remember that he did the same thing about himself. "Preachers, take your ministry seriously," he would say, "but don't take yourself too seriously."

He even had a place for gallows humor—the idea of finding humor in sad situations. Joe would say, "Sometimes you have to laugh to keep from crying."

Abraham Lincoln said, "I laugh because I must not cry. With the fearful strain that is on me night and day, if I did not laugh I should die." Sometimes we preachers need to just lighten up.

Come Apart

Vance Havner once quoted from the KJV about how Jesus told His disciples to come apart and rest and pray. Havner said something such as, "If we don't come apart and rest, we will just come apart."

Joe believed preachers must get away—to try to forget their burdens and concerns with the church and relax for a while. Few realize the stress a pastor goes through. For Joe, relaxation meant fishing or hunting. He used live shrimp to fish for speckled trout (spotted weakfish). He sometimes complained about the high cost for a quart of live shrimp. Then he justified the cost by saying, "It's a lot cheaper than paying $60 an hour for a psychologist." For him, fishing was therapy.

Brumbelow's Advice to Young Preachers

• In your area find an older preacher that you can respect. Become best friends with him. Go to him often for counsel. (On the other hand, Joe remembered the advice of an old pastor, R. G. Commander: "Make friends with preachers that are younger than you are. The older you get, the fewer contemporaries you have with whom to fellowship." Joe thought that being friends with the younger staff at FBC, Lake Jackson was a privilege.

• Attend associational meetings and conventions. Sometimes they might be boring, but you need the fellowship. A preacher needs fellowship with other preachers. You can talk to them about things you can't talk to anyone else about. Also, at these meetings conservative pastors need to be present, supportive, and vote their convictions. You also can get some good sermon and illustration material and pastoral help from those meetings.

• Put God first, your family second, and your church third.

• When you go to a new church, preach a series on 1 Corinthians. It covers just about every problem you can have in a church.

• A pastor's job is to comfort the afflicted and afflict the comfortable.

44

• If a sick person wants to talk about death and heaven, let the person do so. Early in his ministry Joe avoided the issue and said something like, "You're going to outlive me." He realized he was avoiding talking about death and heaven—not because it made the patient uncomfortable, but because Joe was uncomfortable. After that, he let the patient take the lead. If the patient wanted to talk about those things, Brother Joe would be glad to do so.

• Believe in, preach, and teach the Bible and the fundamental doctrines of the faith. Basic doctrines such as the divine inspiration and inerrancy of the Bible; the Trinity; the Deity of Jesus; Salvation only through personal faith in Jesus Christ; Jesus' death on the cross for our sins; Jesus' literal, bodily resurrection; the literal return of Christ to the earth; the resurrection; judgment; heaven, and hell.

• Study and be prepared when you preach. (Joe said, "Never tell the congregation how unprepared you are, because they will soon find out.") Preach the Word of God; use illustrations and humor. Make your sermons interesting and easy to understand. Joe used both expository (verse-by-verse) and topical preaching.

• Preach the importance of soul-winning; practice it in your personal life.

• Be familiar with the lives of great Christian preachers, missionaries, etc.

• Make a big deal out of special days such as Homecoming Day and revivals. Make a big deal out of someone getting saved. After all, the Bible says "there is joy in the presence of the angels of God over one sinner that repenteth" (Lk. 15:10 KJV).

• Love your people. Visit them, pray for them. Love those that are difficult to love. Especially pray for the ones that give you a rough time. It helps them. Perhaps more importantly, it helps you. Sometimes Joe referred to a cantankerous member by saying, "I sure pray a lot for him".

• Know what we believe as Christians and as Baptists. Know why we believe it. (A good place to start is with the Baptist Classics series published by Broadman & Holman. It has sermons and biographies from such leaders as B. H. Carroll, R. G. Lee, etc.)

• You can accomplish an amazing amount if you don't care who gets the credit. Throw out an idea; let someone else run with it. Be happy for that person to get all the credit as long as the job gets accomplished.

• Support and encourage your staff. One of many things Joe admired about his pastor, Dr. John Hatch, was how gracious he was with his staff. Brother John never felt threatened, as some pastors do, when an individual or the church complimented a staff member.

• Don't be a hypocrite. You won't be perfect, but be sincere and live what you preach. Pray often; rely on the Lord.

• Brother Joe, in weddings and funerals, often used *The Pastor's Manual* by J. R. Hobbs and Criswell's *Guidebook for Pastors,* both published by Broadman Publishers.

Letting Young Preachers Preach

If a young man surrendered to the ministry in Brother Joe's church, he gave him the chance to preach. He believed that a pastor was to give the preacher boys in his church that opportunity. He remembered what Harvey Graham had done through the years. Harvey gave his preachers the chance to preach—so much so that some of his church members began to complain. So Brother Harvey started a Preacher-Boys' Revival. Every preacher who attended got the opportunity to preach. Several preached in each service, so he would limit them to 10 or 15 minutes each. The Preacher Boys' Revival was a great help in starting and encouraging the ministries of numerous preachers. Some would be amused at "preacher boys" in their 50s and 60s that continued to participate through the years.

Brother Joe also emphasized to preachers the importance of their finding opportunities to preach. A young preacher can preach, for example, in a nursing home. Many laymen and women lead out in weekly and monthly worship services and are

46

looking for preachers to preach or bring devotionals. When I was a teen-ager, Mrs. Osea Voelkle invited me to preach at a couple of the nursing home services she led in Houston. Young preachers can gain a wealth of experience, if not monetary income, in taking such opportunities.

Joe told the story (I think he got it from his good friend, evangelist Bill Klinglesmith) about the time he preached a revival in a nursing home. He said, "We had a great service. There wasn't a dry seat in the house."

Grapenuts®

Joe sometimes spoke strongly about those whom he believed to be in error—those who strayed from the Bible as their final authority. He said about one such group, "Christian Science is like Grapenuts. The cereal Grapenuts® is not grapes, and it's not nuts. Christian Science is not Christian, nor is it science."

One More Point

As Joe concluded a sermon, he sometimes said, "As the fat woman said while climbing through a barbed-wire fence, 'One more point, and I'm through.'"

On Short Sermons

Joe's friend from college, East Texas Baptist University (ETBU) professor Franklin Atkinson, said, "There is no such thing as a bad short sermon."

Sometimes a service would run long before Joe got up to preach. In such instances the preacher usually is blamed, no matter how short he then keeps his message. Sometimes Joe would say, "If you will listen fast, I'll preach fast."

On other occasions he was known to say, "As Elizabeth Taylor told her last husband, 'I won't keep you long.'"

Chapter 3

If the Barn Needs Painting

Some have pointed to 1 Peter 3:3-5 and taught that a woman is not to wear jewelry or makeup. Joe pointed out that the Scripture is not banning these things, just teaching that a Christian woman's beauty is to originate from within, not solely from outward ornaments.

Should a woman wear makeup? Joe would say, "If the barn needs painting, I think you ought to paint it."

Long Hair and Flat Tires

Joe ministered during the hippie days and consistently taught biblical values and morality, regardless of whether doing so was popular. The fashion of men wearing long hair became stylish; Joe preached against it. Using 1 Corinthians 11 he believed that long hair was a shame for a man. He encouraged men and women to be proud of their gender and look like it.

Joe never went as far as some to make detailed rules and measurements about how long is long, but he believed that if someone has to look at you a second time to figure out whether you are a man or a woman, you're probably violating this Scripture.

He told of stopping to help a woman who was trying to change a flat tire. She had long, pretty hair and was down on her knees with her back to him. He walked up and said, "Ma'am, can I help you with your flat tire?" "She" turned around; Joe saw a beard and mustache. The person said no help was needed; Joe made himself scarce.

The Anvil

I stood one evening by the blacksmith's door
And heard the anvil ring the vesper chime,
And looking in I saw upon the floor
Old hammers worn with years of beating time.

"How many anvils have you had," said I,
"To wear and beat these hammers so?"
"Just one," the blacksmith said with twinkling eye,
"The anvil wears the hammers out, you know."

And so methought the anvil of God's Word
For ages skeptic blows have beat upon,
And though the sound of clanging blows is heard,
The anvil is unharmed, the hammers gone.
—unknown

Bible Not Out of Date

Years ago a converted African cannibal sat under a tree reading his Bible. A European trader passed by and asked him what he was doing. "Reading the Bible," the cannibal replied. "That book is out of date in my country," said the trader. "If it had been out of date here," said the African man, "you would have been eaten a long time ago."

Where Do You Live?

When Brother Joe was pastor of West Heights Baptist in Corpus Christi, he visited in the neighborhood. As he walked from one house to another, he saw a little boy and began talking to him. He was not sure in which house the boy lived. "Where do you live?" the pastor asked the little fellow. "At the Day Care Center, " the boy replied. Brother Joe said he didn't know whether to laugh or cry.

Every Sermon Is Better

On the way out of a Sunday-morning worship service a woman told her pastor, "Every one of your sermons is better than the next."

How to Invest Your Money

Someone said a father is someone who carries photos in his wallet where his money used to be. Brother Joe never made a big salary; the family sometimes struggled to get by. He often said, "I invested my money in three boys."

He truly invested his money—and even more valuable, his time—in us. In the 9th grade I ran cross-country (a two-mile race) at Burbank Junior High School in Houston. At a city meet, at the last minute we discovered that we did not have transportation for five of the 10 members of the team. We appeared to be out of luck. I asked my dad if he could take us across town to the track meet. He was glad to do so. I then realized that out of a total of 10 guys on the cross-country track team, I was the only one with his dad present. That was one of many times I realized how fortunate I was to have had the parents I had.

Since Dad has been gone, each of us boys has tried to look out for Mom. We've attempted to make sure Dad's investment is bringing a good return.

You Going to Church Today?

Mom and Dad never once asked me or my brothers if we were going to church. Understood in our home was the fact that we were all going to church unless we were seriously ill. If company was there, the guests could go with us or wait for us to return after church. That went for Sunday morning, Sunday evening, and Wednesday evening. It also included every service of a revival and most any other special church events. In addition, Mom had us three boys to dress and get ready for church each of those services. She did it and got us there on time!

Brother Joe recommended this family commitment to church to everyone. Some parents want to let their children decide whether to go to church. They don't want to force them to go. Joe pointed out that good parents don't give their kids a choice about going to school, doing homework, taking a bath, eating the right foods, or brushing their teeth. Yet when the most important area of life is concerned—their eternal destinies—they let them do whatever they want.

One final point. Sending your kids to church is not enough. Going with your kids to church as a family is not enough. Live your Christianity at home. If you are faithful to church, church workers have your kids only three or four hours a week. You have them the rest of the time. Mom and Dad were not perfect, but we never doubted that they loved the Lord, loved us, and loved each other. We never doubted that they were sincere in their commitment to the Lord. They lived it in front of us. "Train up a child in the way he should go, and when he is old he will not depart from it" (Prov. 22:6).

What A Well-Behaved Boy!

Dad did not sit with us in church since he was the pastor. (One thing Bonnie enjoyed later in life, when Joe retired, was getting to sit next to him in church.) In my younger years Mom sat with me in church. She could thump an ear like you wouldn't believe! When my misbehavior in church really got bad, she took me outside. When she did so, brother, it was serious.

When I was 5 or 6, Mom wanted to sing in the choir, but that meant I would sit by myself in church. She had a talk with me and told me to sit on the first or second row. She would sit in the choir where she could see me. If I ever misbehaved, a reckoning awaited. When I started to misbehave, she could give me a look only a mother can give.

People occasionally commented on what a well-behaved boy I was in church. They did not know it was because my life depended on it.

Forgiveness and Qualifications, or Shooting Our Wounded

Brother Joe believed a difference existed between forgiveness and qualifications for a spiritual office. Sometimes a Christian leader commits a scandalous, disqualifying sin. That person has abused his or her position. Some Christians say we should forgive the individual and immediately restore the person to the previous leadership position. If we don't, we are not really forgiving. Joe pointed out that forgiveness, qualifications, and consequences are separate issues. If someone admits and repents of a sin, God will forgive the person. We should forgive, as well. That does not necessarily mean that the individual now is qualified for spiritual leadership. God does not always take away the consequences of our sin. No matter how much a Christian has fouled up, God still can use that Christian but not always in the same leadership position.

Some people accuse the church by saying, "We are the only army that shoots its wounded." Joe liked the quote by evangelist R. L. Sumner, "An army doesn't shoot its wounded, but it does shoot traitors."

Preaching and Politics

Brother Joe never felt led to tell the people from the pulpit for whom to vote in secular politics. He was conservative in his political persuasions. He preached the importance of Christians being informed citizens and voting their convictions. He knew, however, that leading people to the Lord was far more important than was convincing them to vote a party line.

Joe did believe that a preacher should preach to the moral issues of the day. He preached against abortion, liquor, gambling, tobacco, drugs, and for such things as voluntary prayer in schools. But he believed he held a job much more important than did the politician. His primary job was dealing with the destiny of immortal souls. If you win someone to the Lord, that person likely will become a better citizen and voter.

Tobacco

One of the big changes in churches since I was a child concerns the issue of smoking. Although preached against years ago, smoking cigarettes was much more socially acceptable then than it is today. While no one would have thought of smoking in the church building, a common sight was to see men gathered just outside the church entrance smoking before and after church services. You don't see that nearly as much today. Brother Joe used to say, "We would have more people attend, but they can't see the church for the cloud of smoke."

Other related comments from Joe:

"Smoking won't send you to hell; it will just make you smell like you have already been there."

"If God had meant for us to smoke, He would have put a smokestack on the top of our heads."

"A preacher was so against smoking, he used to go around slapping the cigarettes right out of people's mouths and stomping the cigarettes in the ground. The preacher finally died—cancer of the foot."

"Cancer—a cure for smoking."

Brother Joe had a deacon, Lloyd Banes, who stopped smoking. He explained why. He said, "Every time I went to witness to someone for the church, it seemed they were looking right at my shirt pocket (where he kept his pack of cigarettes.)"

Joe did not try to run off smokers; he welcomed them to church. But he believed it was his responsibility to warn of the dangers of smoking. As noted above, he occasionally did so on a humorous note.

Your body is the temple of the Holy Spirit (1 Cor. 6:19-20); don't smoke or do anything to harm it. And remember that never starting to smoke is easier than to start and then stop.

Some Favorite Songs
Only A Sinner Saved By Grace; Ask Ye What Great Thing I Know; The Son Will Still Be Shining In Gloryland; Amazing Grace; What A Friend We Have In Jesus; I Shall Not Be Moved.

What Then?
When the choir has sung its last anthem
And the preacher has voiced his last prayer,
And the people have heard their last sermon
And the sound has died out in the air,
When the Bible lies closed on the altar
And the pews are all empty of men,
When each one stands facing his record,
And the great Book is opened—WHAT THEN?

—J. W. Green

Father Brumbelow?
While visiting in Corpus Christi, Brother Joe ran into a fellow and had a conversation something like this: Joe identified himself as the pastor of West Heights Baptist Church. He asked the man if he knew Jesus. The man replied, "Yes, Father," (a term used for Catholic Priests, not used by Baptists and Evangelicals) "I'm a Baptist."

Deacons
Brother Joe respected and got along well with deacons. He saw times in which godly deacons went out of their way to keep peace in the church and support their pastor. But Joe could not resist giving them a difficult time once in a while. A couple of his stories:

"A pastor walks into an antique shop and sees a little gold mouse. 'What does it do?' he asks. The shopkeeper winds up the little gold mouse; it shakes and sputters. It then rolls out onto the street. Amazingly, every mouse in the neighborhood comes out, following it like the pied piper. The gold mouse leads them down

54

to the river. The mice march right into the river and are swept away. The gold mouse then comes back to the antique shop. The shopkeeper asks, 'Would you like to purchase it?' 'Forget about the gold mouse,' the pastor said, 'do you have a little gold deacon?'"

"A man needed a brain transplant. The doctor said, 'We have three brains available for transplant. A physician's brain for $10,000, a lawyer's brain for $30,000, and a deacon's brain for $100,000.' 'Why is the deacon's brain so much more expensive?' the patient asked. The doctor replied, 'It's never been used.'"

Stranded on Uninhabited Isle

"Two men were stranded on a deserted island. The first begins to wring his hands and cry, 'We're doomed. No one will ever find us here.' The second is relaxed, pulls a coconut out of a tree, cracks it open, and gets a drink. 'How can you be so calm?' the first man demands. 'Don't you know there is no hope? We'll never be found?' The second man assures him, 'Relax. We have nothing to worry about. I'm a multimillionaire. I faithfully go to church and tithe my income each Sunday. My pastor will find me within two weeks!'"

Best Thing A Father Can Do for His Children Is to Love Their Mother

Dad's death was sudden and unexpected. Yet on some level, I think he had a premonition of his death. He sometimes would say, "I'm getting so old, my friends in heaven are beginning to think I didn't make it." Joe also said, "I'm getting so old, I don't even buy green bananas."

We often worked together vegetable gardening and growing and grafting fruit trees. The spring of the year he died, we went to a friend's home to buy a Tropic Sweet peach tree (a variety that does great in the upper Texas Gulf Coast area if you add sharp or coarse sand and plant it in a very well-drained, sunny location). John Panzarella reminded him that a peach tree lives only about 10 or 15 years. Joe laughed and said that was as long as he would need it. (By the way, Joe and Bonnie were able to get six, great-tasting peaches from that tree before Dad went on to be with the Lord.)

Dad always complimented my mother. He did not do it for show. His actions obviously were sincere. During the last few months of his life, however, the compliments became more frequent and somewhat more eloquent. More than once he told me that he did not think my mother had ever done anything wrong in their marriage. He complimented her to me in private, when no one else was around. He wanted me, Mom, and everyone to know how much he loved her. After the funeral, the pastor's secretary, Rita Tedder, told me about one of their staff meetings at the Texas Baptist Encampment in Palacios. She walked by Dad and just in passing heard him talking on his cell phone to Bonnie, who was at home. She said she was so impressed by the tenderness and sincerity of his voice as he talked to his wife.

Mom and Dad never had great wealth to bestow on me. They left me, however, with a priceless Christian legacy and a security that can be found nowhere else than in the unconditional love of your parents for you and for each other.

Whether or not you grew up in such a home, you can do all within your power now to make such a home for your children.

What a Great Testimony

I have about 17 acres of pasture in the Brazoria, TX, area. Mark and I built a house on the property several years ago. It still is only dryed in, with no utilities yet. I plan on finishing the house sometime before I retire. The land is wooded with pecan trees, live oaks, water oaks, hackberries, elms, and about three million palmettos (a dwarf form of a palm tree). We have several cows on it and an occasional horse. Through the last several years Dad and I (and sometimes Mark and his family) have worked on it. We have gardened, planted fruit and nut trees, used a DR Brush Cutter, cleared brush, and fixed barbed-wire fences.

We have also done a little fishing, hunting, and trapping on the property. Dad loved getting out in the country.

Mom and Dad were so close; Dad hated the thought of living without Mom. When Mom had bypass surgery in February, 2000, I heard Dad, with tears in his eyes, say, "I'm afraid I'm going to lose her." God blessed; she got through the surgery fine.

Dad, with a little humor, would tell her, "If you die before I do, I think I'll just go live in David's house out in the country and be a hermit." To that Mom would reply, "That would be a great Christian testimony, wouldn't it?"

Two Ph.D.'s

Brother Joe had an earned bachelor's degree from UCC but did not go to seminary. He had a great amount of respect for those who earned a doctor's degree and still believed the Bible and won others to Christ.

He had a preacher friend who excitedly told him at a pastor's conference, "Joe, I finally done it." "What did you do?" Joe asked. "I finally done it. I got my doctor's degree," he said. Joe congratulated him, though he had doubts about this particular preacher's academic ability. The preacher then went on to say, "Now I'm going to start work on my master's degree." (For those who may be unaware of how higher education works, a person receives a doctorate last, after the bachelor's and master's degrees. This preacher had gotten what many refer to as a mail-order degree rather than an earned one.)

Brother Joe would joke, "I have two Ph.D.'s, but one of them is broken." He then would explain that Ph.D. stood for "post-hole digger." (Ph.D. usually refers to doctor of philosophy—a terminal degree, or the highest academic degree.)

World War II Hero, Sinner, Saint

When he was pastor of Leedale Baptist Church in northeast Houston, Joe visited Mr. "Hoot" Gibson at his home. As usual, Gibson had a beer in his hand. Joe found out that Gibson had been in some of the toughest battles of World War II. Most in his unit did not make it out alive. He had a helmet with a bullet hole in it. The bullet had gone through the front of the helmet and creased around the inside of it without entering his head.

Joe witnessed to him. Gibson eventually asked Jesus to forgive him of his sins and to enter his heart and be his Savior. He became an outstanding Christian man.

Mr. Gibson later said to Brother Joe, "I told you I could hold my liquor. You told me that was the worst kind. People will see you and think, 'If it's alright for him to drink, it's alright for me.' Then the person may end up an alcoholic."

Someone later said of Mr. Gibson, "Every time I saw him, he used to have a can of beer in his hand. Now he won't even let someone on his property with a beer."

One Evening in October
One evening in October
When I was far from sober,
And dragging home a load with manly pride,
My poor feet began to stutter,
So I lay down in the gutter,
And a pig came by and parked right by my side.

Then I warbled: "It's fair weather
When good fellows get together."
When a lady passing by was heard to say:
"You can tell a man who boozes
By the company he chooses."
Then the pig got up and slowly walked away!
—unknown

Practical Jokes
Joe had a great sense of humor and loved practical jokes, even if they were played on him. We had planted a couple of grapevines in his backyard two or three years earlier. In the sum-

58

mer of 2002 the vines had several grape clusters that were not quite ripe. I went to Hobby Lobby and bought a cluster of plastic grapes that looked just like Dad's grapes. I nailed them among the grapes at the top of the arbor. The next morning he was thrilled to see the cluster of ripe grapes and asked me to climb up and pick one. I did. Before he realized they were plastic, he had already popped one in his mouth. I think he laughed more than I did about that practical joke.

Dad's grandson, Daniel, (about 12 then) set some steel foothold traps on my property. Dad and I went early the next morning and found one of his traps without anything in it. We had a beanbag stuffed-animal toy ready and put its foot in the trap. We then scuffed up the area and dragged the trap a few yards away. Later Daniel saw the trap was missing and began to track it. We had a fun time seeing Daniel's reaction to trapping this popular toy.

On another occasion Daniel had planted some watermelons. They had grown up in weeds and had not produced. Dad bought a watermelon and put it in the garden. A week or two later Daniel joyously announced he could grow watermelons after all. We then let him know what really happened.

Daniel and Mark later got us back. We had set a live-catch, wild-hog trap. Up until that time we had never caught a hog. Mark bought a live wild hog and put it in the trap. We told everyone about catching that hog before Mark and Daniel laughingly told what really happened.

Joe had been guilty in the past of playing jokes with hand buzzers, pens that exploded, fake sore fingers, etc. With cardstock paper he would turn a glass of water upside down and leave it on the table in the UCC cafeteria. He loved a good practical joke, even if it was at his expense.

Study Bibles
Some criticize Study Bibles because the readers may give the study notes the same authority as the text of the Bible itself.

Informed Christians, of course, know that biblical inspiration refers to the Bible itself, not to an individual's study notes. The notes and references, however, can help in Bible study. Joe did not always agree with his Study Bible's notes, but he used them often.

Joe always used the *Scofield Reference Bible*. He later also used the *Criswell Study Bible* edited by W.A. Criswell and Paige Patterson.

For years the only Study Bible available was Scofield. It is conservative and premillennial (theological term about the Second Coming of Christ; see chapter 10, *Worthy Is the Lamb*), so those who are not as conservative or not premillennial have been known to dislike it. In his younger days Joe seemed to enjoy taking his Scofield Bible to class to antagonize his amillennial professors. He sometimes goaded them in a friendly way by saying, "That's not what my Scofield Bible says." Joe once quipped, "I believe Jesus is going to return riding a white horse, with a sword in one hand and a Scofield Bible in the other hand."

Red-Letter Edition

Dad and I disagreed on this one, although I admit he had a good point. He never liked a red-letter edition of the Bible. His reasoning, "I believe Jesus wrote it all." He worried that some would place more weight on the words of Jesus and less on the rest of Holy Scripture. He believed that all 66 books of the Bible are inspired and inerrant (Ps. 119:160; John 17:17; 2 Tim. 3:16; 2 Pet. 1:21). This sometimes is called plenary verbal inspiration (plenary—all, the totality of Scripture; verbal—every word of the Bible; inspiration—God inspired the Bible in such a way that it is totally true and trustworthy; it is the very Word of God.) God inspired the Bible in such a way that the words of the human authors also were the words of God.

I disagreed on the issue of Red-Letter Editions (I liked the idea of being able to turn to a Scripture and immediately tell if it was a direct quotation of Jesus.); I agreed completely with him about plenary verbal inspiration and the inerrancy of the Bible.

Identity of the Antichrist

Brother Joe called himself a pretribulational premillennialist. (That did not mean, however, that he thought everyone who disagreed with him on eschatology was a heretic.) He believed that Jesus could return at any moment (this refers to the rapture and the resurrection of the just—John 14:3; 1 Thess. 4:13-18; 1 Cor. 15; etc.). After the rapture would be a seven-year period of great tribulation on the earth. During that time would be the rise of the antichrist. The antichrist would be a world leader who first would offer peace but would be an evil dictator. At the end of this period of tribulation and Armageddon, Christ would return to earth and set up His millennial Kingdom. Jesus, the Prince of Peace, would bring peace on earth.

Just because Joe was a premillennialist did not mean he went along with every extremist who also was premillennial. Many have attempted to set a date for the return of Christ. Joe had more sense than to do so (Matt. 24:36, 42, 44). He saw many of those dates go by. That included the book he received in the mail in 1988 entitled *88 Reasons Christ Will Return in 1988*.

Some also have attempted to figure out who is the antichrist. Joe did not believe that would become apparent until after the rapture. Through the years Hitler, the pope, Stalin, Kennedy, Clinton, and others have been accused of being the antichrist.

In the early 1970s Henry Kissinger was accused by some of being the antichrist. His accusers derived a numerical formula. For your edification it is listed here: Take the 26 letters of the alphabet. Give each letter a number from one to 26 (A=1, B=2, and so on). Now see what the name Kissinger adds up to. (Don't include his first name—Henry—because it doesn't work that way!). Multiply it by 6 and you get 666. The mark of the beast is 666 (Rev. 13:18). Now you have it. The accusers had proven their case.

Hold on a minute! Brother Joe pointed out that you can derive some numerical formula to make anyone's name equal 666. Take Brumbelow, for instance! Using the same formula, he pointed out that Brumbelow also equals the same number. Yet I think one can prove that Joe Brumbelow was not the antichrist!

The Day Joe Brumbelow Lost His Faith

We sometimes use the word *faith* to refer to our system of beliefs as Christians—the basic truths taught in the Bible, the faith of our fathers. That faith will not change or end.

We also use *faith* to refer to our trust that God is true to His promises. That kind of faith will not last forever. On more than one occasion Dad personally talked with me about this. "Faith is the substance of things hoped for, the evidence of things not seen" (Heb. 11:1). When you have those things, when you see those things, faith no longer is necessary. Brother Joe told of how one day Abraham lost his faith. One day Moses and Elijah lost their faith. When we get to heaven, our faith will end in the reality of the things God has prepared for us. Faith is one virtue that we will not need in heaven. As the song *Beulah Land* so aptly says, "Where my faith will end in sight." That is why Paul said, under the inspiration of the Holy Spirit, "Now abide faith, hope, love, these three; but the greatest of these is love" (1 Cor. 13:13). On August 30, 2002, Brother Joe Brumbelow lost his faith.

Preachers and Fried Chicken

Years ago, every time you attended a church dinner on the grounds, virtually every family brought homemade fried chicken. Now the only time you see it at church is when it has been purchased from a fast-food establishment.

When homemade fried chicken was so popular, everyone joked about how preachers loved it. How could you be a Baptist preacher unless you like fried chicken?

During those days Joe preached a revival in Kerrville. Also common during a revival in those days was the fact that the evangelist ate in a church member's home at least once each day. Every time that week he and Bonnie would go to a home to eat, the folks would begin with, "We know how preachers like fried

62

chicken." Joe loved fried chicken, but sometimes you have had your fill. Day after day, for five solid days, it was fried chicken. By the end of the revival Joe and Bonnie were sick of fried chicken. At the end of the week, Joe said no chicken was left in the whole town of Kerrville. He did say that as they were leaving, they saw a chicken on the outskirts of town, and it was running.

Brother Joe

Baptist preachers usually will answer to just about anything. They are called preacher, pastor, Dr., Mr., by their first name, and maybe by a name or two that can't be mentioned in this book.

Joe most commonly was known as "Brother Joe." This term is not as common today. What's behind it? Christians know that believers are brothers and sisters in Christ (John 1:12; Phil. 2:25; Col. 4:7, 9; Rom. 16:1). In earlier days Baptists and other Christians commonly referred to persons in their membership as Brother John, Sister Ruth, etc. For some reason *brother* seemed to remain in use longer than did *sister*. While Baptists believe in respecting and honoring their pastor, they never have made a large distinction between clergy and laity. We all have equal access to God (Heb. 4:14-16). Joe liked the simple title "Brother Joe."

Baptists believe in two Scriptural church offices today: pastors and deacons. Other offices, of course, are used in churches, but these are the two specifically mentioned in the Bible. In New Testament times the office of pastor was referred to by three terms; pastor, bishop, and elder. *Pastor* literally means shepherd. *Bishop* means overseer. *Elder*—pastors usually were older, although this began to be used as a term of respect for any pastor, even the younger ones. A hundred or so years ago Baptists commonly called their pastor "Elder Smith."

Notice in the Bible that at times it says "with the bishops and deacons" (Phil. 1:1). It never says "greet the elders and bishops"; that would be redundant.

Chapter 4

Redeemed

Redeemed means to be bought back. That is a biblical term (1 Pet. 1:18-19, etc.) that tells what Jesus Christ did for us as He died for our sins on the cross of Calvary. God in His righteousness could not ignore our sins. So Jesus took our punishment. He bought us back from our sins—from Satan's clutches.

Joe told the story of an old-time preacher, Dr. A. J. Gordon, of Boston. One day, when he was tired from study, Dr. Gordon went for a walk. He met a boy carrying a cage full of sparrows. "Son, where did you get those birds?" "I trapped them." "What are you going to do with them?" "Me and my friends are going to play with them." "What are you going to do when you get tired of playing with them?" "I guess we'll just feed them to the cats."

The preacher looked at those helpless little birds. They were frightened, on the floor of the cage.

The preacher then asked, "Son, will you sell them to me?"

"Preacher, you don't want them."

"Never mind, son. Will you sell them to me?"

"Preacher, they're not canaries. They can't sing or do nothing."

"I know. Will you still sell them to me?"

The boy hesitated and then said, "I'll take two dollars for them and the cage, too."

Dr. Gordon paid the boy and took the cage and birds. The boy looked at the preacher as if he had lost his mind.

When the preacher was alone, he opened the cage and let the sparrows fly out, one by one. The next day in his sermon the preacher said that it seemed that as the birds flew away they sang, "Redeemed! Redeemed! Redeemed!"

Once upon a time Satan carried a cage. In that cage was the whole of the human race. Jesus asked the devil, "What do you have there?"

"A cage full of sinners."

"What are you going to do with them?"

"I'm going to play with them for a while."

"What are you going to do when you get tired playing with them?

"I'm going to send them to hell."

Jesus said, "Lucifer, I'm going to redeem them. I'm going to buy them back."

"You don't want them. They don't care about You. They just care about themselves. They will spit in Your face. They'll crucify You."

"But I still love them. I'm willing to die for them."

So Jesus paid the ultimate price for sinners. He who knew no sin was made sin for us, that we might be made the righteousness of God. Jesus shed His blood on Calvary in our place and rose again. God so loved the world that He gave His only begotten Son to redeem lost humanity from the clutches and slavery of Satan. Those who have accepted what Jesus did for us on the cross of Calvary—we have been redeemed.

The Old Preacher

An old preacher once was asked, "Do you really believe all the Bible?" "No," the preacher replied, "I don't suppose I do. If I did, I'd be a much better man than I am."

The Biggest Lie

A preacher encountered a group of boys and a dog. "What are you doing?" he asked. The boys said, "We're having a contest to see who can tell the biggest lie. Whoever tells the biggest lie gets to keep the dog."

The preacher got red in the face and exclaimed, "Why, that is terrible. That's terrible. In all my life I never would even think of telling a lie."

The boys huddled for a few moments of deliberation. "OK," they said, "You win. You get the dog."

Churchill and the Cup of Tea

Joe appreciated fast, witty retorts. One of his favorites: "The story has been attributed to Winston Churchill that a woman became angry with him. 'If I were your wife, I would put poison in your tea,' she said. Churchill replied, 'Madam, if you were my wife, I'd drink it.'"

Growing Up in the Hill Country

Central Texas has some beautiful, rugged hills and is known as the Hill Country. Joe, however, grew up in Damon on the Gulf Coast. The Gulf Coast area of Texas is flat—no hills at all. Except at Damon. Damon Mound is recognized as the only hill in that part of the country. So Joe used to quip that he grew up in the Hill Country.

Running with a Walking Cane

In Corpus Christi Joe realized he needed more exercise and determined to start jogging. Before long he decided that running was not for him and started walking instead. He also would take the stairs instead of the elevator when he visited hospitals.

When he first started running, however, he took a walking cane to protect himself from any dogs as he ran. He mentioned to me that he might look a little foolish running with a walking cane. I replied, "Folks will probably think you just got out of a healing service."

Leaving the SBC

At one point during the conservative resurgence in the SBC a high-profile, more liberal preacher left the SBC to join a more liberal denomination. Joe mused, "That will raise the conservative level of both denominations."

Ramblers and Cadillacs

Years ago an evangelist who led a revival for Brother Joe publicly reproved the people for not taking care of their pastor. He had good intentions, but he ended up hurting instead of helping. The evangelist arrived at the meeting driving an old, second-hand Cadillac. Joe found out that it did not even have a spare tire. But it was a Cadillac, nonetheless. Joe and Bonnie had just bought a brand new Rambler, an American Motors economy car.

The evangelist said, "I can't believe you people don't take better care of your pastor. Here he is, driving an economy car!"

Joe then had to put out some fires and let the people know he was happy and had not instigated what the evangelist said. Joe later would say, "I would rather have had my new Rambler than three of those old, beat-up Cadillacs."

Honeybees

At various times Mark and I have raised honeybees. We started out with log-gum hives and then to movable-frame hives. Dad always had a deathly fear of bees, but as a good father he dutifully helped us work with and rob bees. He told us how his dad, Eldridge Perry (Bud) Brumbelow, would rob bee trees—literally scraping the bees off his arm—and be pretty much unaffected. Dad did not inherit that trait.

Bees tend to become agitated when they are worked with. The worst thing that can happen is for a honey bee to begin crawling up your pants leg. You know you're going to get it; you just don't know when. Sometimes even when you're standing a good ways off, which Dad usually did, they can still locate you They will light on you or start buzzing you. When bees angrily buzz about you, they usually are used to flying at a certain level above ground. If they are buzzing your head, you can squat down or bend over and run; sometimes they will lose track of you. In the 1990s Mark and I had moved a hive of bees to my property. They were agitated; Dad was standing a good ways off. You could see the bees angrily patrolling the area. I could not resist easing up behind Dad with a twig and brushing his hair and neck. He tensed up, stooped down, bent over, and ran across the pasture. It was a sight to behold. When you get to heaven, ask to see the videotape!

Dad used a great illustration about honeybees. A honey bee has a barbed stinger. It only can sting one time, because the stinger either will be pulled out completely in your skin or will be pulled and damaged enough that the bee cannot sting again and will soon die. Once an individual honeybee has stung you, it never can hurt you again.

A mother and daughter were picking blackberries. A honeybee began buzzing around the little girl. "I'm afraid, Mommy," she said. The mother replied, "You have nothing to be afraid of." "Why?" the girl asked. "It can sting me." "No, it can't," the mother said. She then showed the girl her hand with the stinger of that honeybee still embedded. "The bee's stinger broke off in me and never can hurt anyone again."

In 1 Corinthians 15:55 (KJV) Paul said, "O death, where is thy sting? O grave, where is thy victory?" The sting of death broke off in Jesus when He died for your sins and mine. Jesus conquered death by rising again. When we trust Jesus and His sacrifice for us on the cross, death will be swallowed up in victory.

Humility
Humility is illusive. If you have it, you don't know it. When you think you have it, you've lost it. When Joe preached on humility, he told about the man who wrote the book, *My Humility and How I Attained It.*

Simon Peter and Racism
Brother Joe dealt well with racism. He believed that Jesus loved all of humanity and died for everyone (1 John 2:2; John

3:16; Acts 10:34-35; 1 Tim. 2:3-6; 4:10; etc.). He wanted his church to be open to everyone regardless of race or background. As much as possible, all are to be treated equally.

He recognized that racists of all colors existed. He also recognized that some otherwise good Christians had a problem with prejudice. Sometimes the question is not whether you are prejudiced but how you deal with those feelings and whether you are willing to acknowledge that they are wrong.

One woman in his church probably was the biggest supporter of the Southern Baptist Lottie Moon Christmas Offering for the International Mission Board (then the Foreign Mission Board). She also was the most opposed to those of another race attending her church. Joe considered ironic the fact that she so wanted our missionaries to go to other countries and win the people there to the Lord but wanted to let those of other races in America go to hell. When Joe baptized a young black man (this was about 1970), she and her husband left the church.

A year or two later she talked to Brother Joe about how she missed her church and wanted to return. He told her she was welcome but that nothing had changed at the church since she had been gone. She returned anyway.

More than one Christian acknowledged to him that they were prejudiced, but they knew it was wrong and wanted to do right. Joe sent one such man to visit Mrs. Lizzie Guidry. Mrs. Guidry was an older black woman who lived at the back of Oxford Place, the low-rent, government apartments that bordered the church. Mrs. Guidry was poor but dressed to perfection every time she attended church. She had as loving and sweet a Christian attitude as anyone could have. She won this man over in one visit. He often visited her. When he greeted her at church, he always did so with a hug. She never had even discussed the issue of prejudice. A loving Christian attitude by someone of any race can do more to curb prejudice than can 10 seminars.

Does hope exist for the prejudiced? During this period Brother Joe realized that Simon Peter was a racist when he preached on the Day of Pentecost and 3,000 souls were saved (Acts 2). Some time later, in Acts 10, God dealt with Peter's racism. That is not meant to justify prejudice; just to say that God takes us where we are and then leads us to where we ought to be. If Peter had not been willing to give up his prejudice, Brother Joe did not believe that God would have continued to use him in such a mighty way. God even loves people who are prejudiced. And prejudiced people can change.

A Spiritual Nap
When anyone gets tired and grouchy, being spiritual is almost impossible. Hence the joke around our house: Sometimes the most spiritual thing you can do is take a nap.

Broken Record
Younger folks don't know the meaning of a broken record. For years vinyl records were the standard. Sometimes a record would have a scratch or break in it. When the needle playing the record hit the scratch, it would jump back and play the same word or phrase over and over.

Brother Joe believed that salvation was by faith alone in Christ alone by grace alone. So many today are trying in one way or another to work their way to heaven.

When preaching on Ephesians 2:8-9 (KJV) Joe said, "I wish I could put this on a record and break the record. It would play, 'For by grace are ye saved through faith; and that not of yourselves: it is the gift of God: not of works . . . not of works . . . not of works . . . not of works . . . not of works . . .'"

Jesus Paid a Part?
When preaching about salvation by grace, not by works, Joe used the following example: "Those who teach that salvation is by works should change the hymn *Jesus Paid It All* to read,
          'Jesus paid a part,
          Some to Him I owe.

Sin hath left a crimson stain,
We washed it white as snow.'"

Greek and the Holy Land

Some preachers get a little carried away with Greek (the
original language of the New Testament portion of the Bible) and
want to carefully explain every word in the original language in
excruciating detail. Joe confessed that he knew very little Greek.
He barely survived Greek class in college. About the only Greek
words he knew were *baptizo* and *anna eklesia* (the last two
words from his college friend named Upchurch. In Joe's year-
book he signed his name Anna Eklesia).

Some preachers also get overly enthusiastic about visiting the
Holy Land and tell about it in every sermon. Joe always wanted
to go to Israel but never did. He finally concluded that he would
just have to wait and visit the Holy Land during the millennium.

He told of one church that tired of preachers spouting Greek
and Holy Land references. This church's pulpit committee had
two criteria for their next pastor: he must not know Greek and
must have never been to the Holy Land.

How to Have Revival

Brother Joe never believed revival meetings had become out-
dated. He often used evangelists, pastors, and singers in revival.
Some said, "Revival doesn't last." He replied, "Neither does a
bath, but it does you a lot of good."

A revival is a series of meetings with preaching and singing.
Worship services usually begin with both services Sunday and
each night of the week through Wednesday or however long a
church desires. Revivals sometimes include noon services as
well. The purpose is to revive the saints and to win the lost to
Christ.

Brother Joe usually had revival meetings in his church at
least once a year. He occasionally held other meetings such as
the January Bible Study.

How do you have a revival? Some of his basics:

1. Publicize the revival heavily for at least two or three weeks before the meeting. Make it the most important thing in your life and in the life of the church. Emphasize the importance of each member being present at every service and bringing someone. Mail letters to church members, visitors, prospects, etc. about the revival.

2. Have professionally prepared revival flyers to mail out and for the church members to give out. Put the flyers on bulletin boards and in store windows. Send a flyer, a photo, and a press release to area newspapers and radio stations. Send the information early to the state Baptist papers and the associational office. Send flyers to area churches.

3. In services leading up to the meeting preach on the importance of revival.

4. Pray for revival. (Sometimes he had cottage prayer meetings or divided up groups at church to pray for revival.) Joe said three things are necessary to have true revival: First, pray. Second, pray. Third, pray.

5. Visit and pray for the lost and the backslidden.

6. Have special nights for the revival: Youth pizza supper, pre-teen hot dog supper, pack the pew night, etc.

Joe tried not to wear out the evangelist visiting during the revival. Do 90 percent of the work of the revival before the evangelist arrives, but some key visits can be made during the week.

Take good care of the evangelist during the week. Most evangelists prefer a motel room for convenience and privacy. Don't get the cheapest motel. Take care of his meals and any other incidentals. Pay for his travel expense (and don't take it out of the love offering.)

Early in Joe's ministry he put the evangelist's love offering in the church budget, because he was afraid a freewill offering would not be sufficient. Then he discovered if the people knew to what they were giving, and that the church had no budgeted item to take care of it, the love offering would be much more.

At every service of the revival Brother Joe explained that every penny received for the revival offering would go to the evangelistic team. He explained how for many evangelists the love offering was their only or major means of support. The expenses (publicity, motel, travel, etc.) of the revival would be the only church-budgeted items. When you deal with the budget, the pastor can explain to the church the importance of revival and the need to include revival expenses in the yearly budget.

If a smaller church cannot afford all of the expenses, be up-front with the evangelist about it and do the best you can. You may want to get an evangelist in the area who doesn't have to travel so far. If the revival is publicized well, the people like the evangelist and pastor, and the love offering is explained, the church almost always will have a good offering. If you have an outstanding offering, thank God and the people for it. That will help the evangelist during other revivals when he receives very small offerings.

Joe was also careful about giving the evangelist his love offering before he left on the last night of the revival. That means having the ushers and treasurer ready to count the offering and write a check immediately after the last service. The evangelist probably needs it as soon as possible.

Revivals are important and still are greatly used of God.

Bad Evangelists
Many pastors have had a bad experience with an evangelist. He emphasized the offering too much. He made comments that hurt the ministry of the church and pastor. He pitted the youth against the adults or vice versa. He led them into some new, weird doctrine. He was a smart-aleck. During the invitation he put too much pressure on the people (i.e. If you love your mother, you will walk down this aisle. If you ever have had doubts about your salvation, you need to get saved right now. And if you have never doubted your salvation, you really need to get saved!)

73

Joe advised checking with other pastors about the evangelist. Also, if you have a bad experience, don't stop having revivals; just don't get that individual evangelist again.

If you are an evangelist, remember that you are there to help, not hurt, the pastor and the church. The pastor has to live with the situation in which you leave it when the revival ends. That church has some great, humble saints of God; treat them as such.

On the other hand, the people can benefit from hearing preaching that is somewhat different from the pastor's. Evangelists do sometimes say things differently—conduct invitations differently. As pastor don't be overly sensitive or intimidated by such. The pastor will have the people to preach to the rest of the year!

Don't be intimidated when the people compliment the evangelist for his preaching. If the evangelist can't preach, getting him to conduct a revival wasn't a good idea. If the evangelist can preach, join the people in commending the preaching.

Why Doesn't Pastor Snodgrass Get Me to Preach?

Evangelist, don't feel slighted if a good preacher friend of yours does not ask you to preach a revival for him. Don't pressure him about getting you. Joe had some dear preacher friends—evangelists and pastors—whom he never got to preach a revival for him. He loved them and believed in them. He just never felt God leading him to get them to preach a revival.

Be friends with every pastor you can. Send out brochures. But allow God to lead the pastor in who he gets to preach.

Of course, on the other hand, your pastor friend may not be asking you to preach because he doesn't think you could preach your way out of a wet paper bag!

The Blessing

As I was writing this, I attended a revival at Central Baptist Church in Baytown. As I left the service, the evangelist, editor Bill Merrill of *SBC Life*, a Southern Baptist newsmagazine, told me what a blessing my dad had been in his life. He had not known Dad well, but he said that in the few contacts he had with him, Dad impressed and encouraged him.

Since then, at First Baptist Church, Damon, TX, Travis Beard told of how the best revival he ever held was when Joe Brumbelow preached a revival for him in Del Rio, TX. W. D. Kilsby told us at that same Homecoming Day (2004) at Damon that at his church in Cedar Lane, TX, a testimony meeting was held. Three individuals stood and referred to the influence Brother Joe Brumbelow had on their lives.

He said, "That is something for a church in which Brother Joe never preached."

Several years ago a man told me, "You don't know me. Your dad doesn't know me. But your dad was a great influence on my life. Years ago, I watched him and was moved by his convictions, his ministry, and his compassion for the lost."

My brothers and I could tell many other variations of these stories. Over and over, preachers and others have told us what a blessing Dad was to them. How it encourages us to hear that!

To the dads reading this page, are you leaving that kind of legacy for your kids? You can if you get serious about living for God and loving your family.

Christmas Lights

As a staff member at First Baptist Church, Lake Jackson, Brother Joe had the privilege of preaching in the church's Wednesday-night service each week. On a Wednesday after Christmas he said, "The other night I saw the most beautiful Christmas lights I've ever seen. They were the taillights of my kids' cars as they were going home."

Soul-Winning Is What It's All About

A preacher friend, at that time in his mid to late 50s, said, "Joe, I've discovered the secret to ministry. Soul-winning is what it is all about."

Joe heartily agreed but later mentioned it was a shame that this preacher took all those years to discover this truth. Joe wanted soul-winning to be a preacher's passion when he is 20 and when he is 70. "He that winneth souls is wise" (Prov. 11:30 KJV).

The Infallible Word

"I believe the Bible to be the infallible, inspired word of God written by men of old and new through the leadership of God's power and Spirit."—Evangelist Dan Vestal in his book, *Golden Hours in the Bible*, King Publishing, Waco, Texas; 1971, p. viii.

Communism

Did you hear of the man who so rabidly fought communism that he thought a communist was behind every bush and that some of the bushes were communist?

Communism has caused more deaths in the 20th century worldwide than has any other political system. Bible-believing American pastors recognized the great danger it posed and preached against it. Joe was approached by a member of a strongly anti-communist organization and was asked to join. He respectfully declined. The man asked him if he truly wanted to oppose communism. Joe replied, "I'm already a member of the biggest anti-communist organization in the world." Interested, the man asked the name of the organization. Joe said, "The Christian Church." True Christianity and its emphasis on God-given rights and the sanctity of human life has done more to fight the evils of our day than has any human or political organization.

(Joe used the term *Christian Church* not to refer to one denomination but to all of those individuals who have placed their personal faith in Jesus Christ as Lord and Savior and try to live according to the Bible.)

I Think Jesus Was a Good Man, a Great Teacher

Joe realized that the central part of our faith is, "Who is Jesus? Is He God? Is He the only Savior?" Throughout his min-

76

istry Joe was told by some who wanted to sound educated and reasonable without committing themselves, "I think Jesus was a good man—perhaps the greatest who ever lived." Or, "Jesus was a great teacher. We should follow His teachings. They would conclude by saying, "But I don't think Jesus is God or that He is the only way to get to heaven."

Joe would point out that since Jesus claimed to be God and claimed to be the only way to heaven, if He is not, then He is not a good man. If Jesus is not the only way to heaven, then He was a charlatan. Some have put it this way: "Jesus either is Lord, a lunatic, or a liar." Brother Joe would explain that Jesus claimed to be God and accepted worship that is to be given only to God. Jesus Himself said that He was the only way to heaven (Passages from the Bible showing this include: Isa. 9:6; John 1:1, 14; 8:58; 14:6,9; 10:30; 17:5; 20:28-29; Acts 4:12; Rom. 9:5; Titus 2:13; etc.).

We do not have the option of just believing that Jesus was a good man. He either is God, or He is not a good man. He either is the only Savior of the world, as He claimed, or He was lying or deceived. But if Jesus is who He says He is, and who the Bible says He is, then the only way to have your sins forgiven and to be made right with God is by personally trusting Jesus as your Lord and Savior. God makes the rules, not you or me.

This brings to mind a humorous, if sad, thing Joe heard years ago on the radio. A heretical preacher told of receiving a letter from someone in New Orleans saying he had been saved. The preacher said, "Huh, how could he have been saved? I haven't been to New Orleans."

Praise God!
Praising God is expected of us. Some preachers, however, use terms such as "Praise God", "amen", "bless God", and "Hallelujah" a little too often. Sometimes, by mistake, I'm sure, they use them in inappropriate ways. The following are two examples that Joe said he honestly heard on the radio:

"You're going to hell, praise God."

"The devil has been on my coattail all week long, bless his holy name."

Sad Case of the Waders

Joe was an intelligent man. But sometimes we all get caught not thinking. In Houston he was getting rid of some unwanted items including a leaky pair of waders, which he had used for wade-fishing. A man who was not exactly known for his great intellect stopped by. The man asked Joe if he wanted the waders. "No," Joe replied. The man asked, "Are you sure you don't want them?" "No," Joe said, "and you probably don't want them, either. They have leaks in them. They're no good."

When he was sure Joe did not want them, he took out his pocket knife and cut the boots off the rest of the waders. Immediately, the man had a fine new pair of rubber boots. Joe could not believe it. He always was needing rubber boots, but he never had thought of cutting the boots off a bad pair of waders. At the same time, Joe could not bring himself to take back the boots from the fellow to whom he had just given the waders. For the rest of his life he regretted giving away such a fine pair of rubber boots!

Sleeping in Church

Every preacher is a little unsettled about someone who sleeps during his preaching. A person sleeps for various reasons. He or she is tired, bored, had a difficult week, has a health problem, is on medication, etc. One preacher said he believes that the sleeping person is giving the preacher a vote of confidence that he is not going to say anything too out of line in his sermon.

When pastor of Leedale Baptist Church, Houston, Joe had a member who seemed to go to sleep every time Joe preached. That bothered him. At that time, in the 1960s, Billy Graham preached a crusade in Houston, TX, at the Astrodome. Joe's church participated. The same woman went to sleep during Billy

Graham's preaching. After that Brother Joe did not worry as much about her going to sleep during his preaching.

Joe could laugh at himself. He told the true story of recording one of his Sunday sermons so he could hear and critique it. He said, "I sat down that afternoon to listen to it, turned on the cassette tape, and went sound asleep."

Joe also told of the preacher who dreamed he was preaching. He woke up and found out that he was.

Insomnia

Can't sleep at night? Joe recommended the following: "Start reading your Bible. You'll fall asleep every time." He then confessed, "I don't know if it's the Lord saying, 'I'm proud of you for reading My Word, so I will give you some much-needed rest.' Or if it is the devil saying, 'I had better not keep him up any longer if he is going to read the Bible.'"

Don't Believe Everything You Read, or Even See

Joe was a discerning person. He said, "Don't believe everything you hear. Don't believe everything you read. Don't even believe everything you see. Sometimes we have to investigate to find the truth."

To illustrate, he told of going to a Prince's Drive-In on South Main in Houston in the 1950s. You drove up, parked, and the carhop would come and take your order. Later, of course, she would come back with the order. Your order was on a tray that hooked on the side of the car door when the window was open.

This time the carhop went to another car first. The people in the other car had finished; she took their tray. She then arrived at Joe and Bonnie's car, hung the tray on their door, and got ready to take their order.

Joe immediately said, "Ma'am, please get that tray off my door." The tray had an empty beer bottle on it. He explained, "I'm a Baptist preacher. If people saw that, they would think I was drinking beer." She didn't see the problem. She wasn't very happy about having to remove the tray, put it on the ground, then take his order.

Joe pointed out that if one of his church members had driven by at that moment, that person truthfully could have said that he or she saw Brother Joe with a bottle of beer. But that would not have been the whole truth. Check things out. Be sure before you make accusations.

Guarantee against Alcoholism

Brother Joe issued a statement that, if followed, would absolutely guarantee you never would become an alcoholic. The statement was simple: "Never take that first drink. In so doing, you will save yourself, and those who love you most, a world of heartache." He said, "I'd rather have a rattlesnake in my house than a bottle of beer."

He pointed out that about one out of nine drinkers becomes a problem drinker. He said, "How would you feel if you boarded an airplane and asked how safe it was and the pilot said, 'Very safe. We only lose one out of nine flights'? I think you would choose another airline. We should have the same fear of beverage alcohol" (Prov. 23:29-35; Rom. 14:21).

Internet Links

As mentioned in a later chapter, Joe did not use computers or the Internet. He did, however, enjoy the up-to-date news these provided. I frequently copied news stories to share with him. Some of the sites and magazines he preferred:

bpnews.net—Baptist Press (BP) is the official news agency of the SBC and offers a wealth of current news on missions, doctrinal issues, controversial issues, etc. It also is a great source for research on numerous topics.

sbc.net—portal to all Southern Baptist mission boards, seminaries, and agencies.

sbtexas.com—site of Southern Baptists of Texas Convention. Its paper, *The Texan*, was one of Joe's favorites.

worldmag.com—WORLD Magazine, a weekly, general news magazine from a Christian point of view.

Basics of the Christian Life

This may not be the most exciting article, but it is one of the most important. Joe taught that the secret to the Christian life involves four main areas: First, reading the Bible each day and hiding its words in your heart. If you are new to Christianity, start with the Gospel of John. Then read the other books of the New Testament. Read at least a chapter a day. Second, pray every day. Reading the Bible is a way of God speaking to you. Prayer involves you speaking directly to God. Talk to God about everything. Praise Him, thank Him, pray for others, ask for forgiveness, pray for yourself. If you have a family, pray together as a family on a regular basis. It doesn't need to be long, but it is important. If children are in the home, you may want to get a good children's Bible-story book. But keep your family devotions with your kids short and sweet. Third, be faithful in church attendance—Sunday morning, Sunday night, midweek service. We need all the strength, instruction, and fellowship a local Bible-believing church provides. The church is not perfect. But don't worry too much about that. If it were, you wouldn't be allowed to attend! And that church needs you. Get involved. Fourth, witness to others. If Jesus Christ has made a difference in your life, you have the privilege and responsibility to tell others about Him.

The Christian life has many other aspects, but if you major on these four, the others will fall in place.

Chapter 5

Fire and Wildfire

"When you have revival and the fire of God, you are going to have some wildfire. I had rather have a little wildfire than have no fire at all."—Joe Brumbelow

Where She Belonged

Joe's death was sudden and unexpected. It happened on a Friday. Our family's world seemed as though it had ended. Do you know where Bonnie and her family were the following Sunday morning? They were gathered with God's people in church. Yes, they shed tears, but Bonnie was going to be where she belonged. The same was true that Sunday night and Wednesday night and the weeks and months since.

Some seem to use tragedy as an excuse to stay home. The greater the tragedy, the greater your need to be among your brothers and sisters in Christ. When you don't feel like going to church may be the time you will get the most out of it.

Since Dad's death Bonnie has been asked if she has received counseling. In the formal sense the answer is no. But she receives counseling three times a week by attending, as usual, her church's regular services.

Only a Sinner

Naught have I gotten, but what I received,
Grace hath bestowed it since I have believed;
Boasting excluded, pride I abase—
I'm only a sinner saved by grace!

82

Once I was foolish, and sin ruled my heart,
Causing my footsteps from God to depart,
Jesus hath found me, happy my case—
I now am a sinner saved by grace!

* * * * *

Only a sinner saved by grace!
Only a sinner saved by grace!
This is my story, to God be the glory—
I'm only a sinner saved by grace!

(—James M. Gray, 1851-1935; president of Moody Bible Institute)

Crawfishing

When they were 10 or 12, Joe and his younger brother, Bill, mowed yards and did other work around town to make a little money. They would get about 50 cents to mow a small yard and $1 for a big yard. One woman in town seemed to be more critical and tight with her money than were others. Joe and Bill had had a bad experience or two with her previously.

Joe and Bill were crawfishing one day. For those who have not experienced the joys of crawfishing; you usually put some bait on the end of your line (a little piece of bacon, chicken bone, chicken skin, etc.) and ease it into a ditch full of water. Before long a crawfish will start to chew on it and will not want to let go. You ease the pole up out of the water and onto dry ground or into your bucket. Carefully avoiding the pinchers, you take it off the line and put it in the bucket. (I heard of one boy who told his little brother the crawfish wanted to shake hands with him.)

Joe and Bill were busy with this pursuit when the previously mentioned, stingy woman arrived and asked them if they could do some weeding around her house for her. As they continued crawfishing, Joe allowed as to how they were just too busy and did not have time to work for her.

When Joe Got Saved

When Joe was a 9-year-old boy, God began to speak to him and convict him of his need for salvation. He had heard the story of how we all were sinners (have done things wrong in the eyes of God) and needed a Savior. He knew that the ultimate penalty for our sin was spiritual death and an eternity in Hell. He also knew that God still loved him and sent His only begotten Son, Jesus, to die on the cross of Calvary for his sins.

Can a 9-year-old boy be a sinner? Scripture says, "All have sinned and fall short of the glory of God" (Rom. 3:23). Joe said he had the capacity to be one of the meanest boys around. When we were boys, my brothers and I found his early school report cards. He made fair grades in other subjects. He made F's in conduct! We got a lot of fun out of that.

One Sunday morning at First Baptist Church, Damon, TX God began to convict Joe of his sin. During the time of invitation (when folks are invited to go to the front of the church to trust Jesus as Savior, for prayer, or to make some other public decision for Christ) that morning Joe held back and refused to repent of his sins and accept Jesus. That afternoon he was heartbroken that he had not gotten saved that morning. He was under such conviction that he told the Lord that if He let him live until the Sunday-night worship service, he would trust Jesus then. He felt that he was the worst sinner in the world. By God's grace, the 9-year-old sinner lived until that evening. During that Sunday-evening invitation he walked to the front of the little church building and talked with the pastor, Brother McMinn. Joe bowed his head and asked Jesus to forgive him of his sins and to enter his heart to be his Lord and Savior. That was the most important decision in Joe Brumbelow's entire life.

Joe later was baptized in Big Creek, not far from what is now Brazos Bend State Park.

Mrs. Lartigue and the Mormons

When I was a teen-ager, the Lartigues were faithful, active

members of our church. Mrs. Carmen Lartigue told, as only she could tell it, of the day a couple of Mormon missionaries stopped by her home. She politely explained to them that she knew the Lord and was actively involved in a Baptist church; she was not interested in their teachings or literature. They persisted. She patiently stood for her beliefs.

"Are you married?" they asked. "Yes," she said. "If you follow our teachings, we assure you that when you die, in the next life you will be married to the same man," the Mormons said.

"That's all I need to hear," Mrs. Lartigue said. "Get out of here! I've put up with that man for 30 years. No way I'm going to put up with him for all eternity!"

Mrs. Stephens and the Jehovah's Witnesses

Mrs. Mildred Stephens had lived a rough life until Brother Joe led her to the Lord. She was gloriously saved. One day Brother Joe was visiting her and her family in the Heights area of Houston. She answered a knock on the door. A couple of Jehovah's Witness visitors were there. Mildred kindly but firmly told them she was not interested in what they had to offer. They were very persistent. She finally got rid of them. As she returned to the living room, Joe said, "I thought you dealt with that pretty well. Sometimes you just can't be nice to those folks." Exasperated, she replied, "I'll tell you one thing. If you hadn't been sitting here, I would have gotten rid of them a lot sooner!"

Runaway Donkey in Downtown Damon

As boys of about 10 and 7, Joe and Bill found a man willing to sell them his donkey for $12. They saved their money from mowing yards and doing other tasks and bought it. Their dad, who people in the area called E. P. or Bud, worked for the Sinclair Oil Company.

One day a man arrived at the Sinclair yard in Damon to get rid of a bunch of junk. He put a paint mark on everything he did not want to keep. One such item was a little cart that had been used to carry a fire extinguisher. It was just right to hitch to a donkey. The brothers went to the blacksmith shop and got some discarded wide belts they had used to run machinery. The belts would be just right to make a harness.

E. P. had told them not to hitch up the donkey while he was at work, but they had everything ready and just could not wait any longer. Their house was at the bottom of the hill, right in the middle of Damon. It was right across from Bull's Grocery Store and next to the Post Office. They got in the cart and directed the donkey to go through Damon up the hill. The donkey and cart pulled perfectly. Congratulating themselves, they turned the donkey around to go downhill back to their house.

They never realized that they would need a brake system for the cart—or that going downhill, a metal bar at the front of the cart would run into the back legs of the donkey.

As they began their descent, things began to go wrong. The cart began going faster than the donkey. The metal bar ran into the back legs of the donkey. The donkey would jump and kick the cart, causing the cart to jump up. Then the donkey would go faster to keep the cart from hitting its back legs. The cart would then lurch forward and hit the donkey again. This caused the donkey to jump, kick the cart, and go even faster. This was all downhill. It happened over and over, faster and faster.

Half way down the hill Bill told Joe it was all his and rolled off the backside of the cart. Yes, Bill said it hurt a lot when he hit the ground.

Joe rode it out. Down to the bottom of the hill, across the street, they finally crashed into a picket fence. At that point the donkey, with bleeding hind legs, broke away from the harness and took off running. The donkey later was found about a mile down Highway 36.

Careful Who You Goose
In the early 1970s we took a family trip to Gemco, a large discount store. Dad did not confess to the following until some-

time later: By this time my brother, Mark, though young, was a big fellow. When we got to the store, we all split up while Mom did the shopping. Dad rounded a corner and saw Mark down the aisle leaning over inspecting some merchandise. Dad saw his opportunity and eased up behind Mark and goosed him. To make a good goose you have to slip up behind someone (of the same gender, mind you) and poke or grab them from the backside. In those days Dad excelled in this particular art. He performed the goose perfectly; Mark jumped from surprise.

The only problem—the person he goosed was not Mark. It was a big fellow who, hunched over, looked just like Mark from behind. Dad tried to explain himself and averted a fist fight in the middle of Gemco. Actually, the man later laughed and said he thought it was his kid who had goosed him.

As I said, Dad did not tell us of this until later. We had, however, wondered why, in the middle of Mom's shopping, Dad returned to her and her shopping cart and followed her around like a whipped pup for the rest of the time at Gemco.

Fact, Faith, Feelings

1. Fact must occur first. Christians are not believers in mythology. Our beliefs are based on the fact, the truth of the Bible, God's inspired Word. (See books on accuracy of the Bible by such authors as R. A. Torrey, W. A. Criswell, Josh McDowell, and others.)

2. Faith is only sufficient when placed in something or someone who is factual. Faith in a myth or legend does no good. Our trust is in the real, historical Jesus who died for our sins and literally rose again.

3. Feelings are important and are wonderful, but they are the least important of the three. Like the last car on a train, feelings are the caboose. When you have the caboose in the front of the train, you'll have problems. A married person may feel wonderful emotions toward his spouse; or sometimes he may have negative feelings. The feelings do not change the fact that he is married.

Getting the above in the right order is vital: fact first, faith in what is factual, and then feelings. Fact, faith, feelings.

> Feelings come and feelings go,
> Feelings are deceiving.
> My faith is in the Word of God,
> Naught else is worth believing.
>
> —unknown

Answered Prayer

The Union Baptist Association's pastors conference was held in Houston each Monday morning. The pastors were invited to speak of how things went in the previous day's services. One Monday Brother Joe said, "Brethren, we have had a big problem at our church for some time. I've agonized about it. I've stayed up at night. I've prayed about the problem. I did not know what else to do. I want you to know that yesterday God answered my prayers. She joined another church!"

A Nickel on the Sidewalk

Often at Monday's pastors conference pastors gave glowing reports of how many attended their church the previous Sunday morning, how many were saved or baptized, or some other positive church reports.

One particular Monday things were unusually quiet. No one said anything during report time. It must have been a dismal Sunday all over Houston. Pastors were asked again, "Doesn't anyone have anything good to say about Sunday?" Finally, Brother Joe stood and said, "Yesterday on my way to church, I found a nickel on the sidewalk." Everyone enjoyed a laugh.

Dr. Hinton, president of Houston Baptist University, was the pastors conference speaker that day. In his message he told about how the school wanted to help preachers' kids financially so they could attend college. He said, "Even this preacher who found a nickel on the sidewalk, if his kids want to attend HBU, we'll make sure they can." More laughter ensued.

Several years later, Joe reminded Dr. Hinton of that statement. I attended HBU my entire freshman year without paying for anything except textbooks. Dr. Hinton made good on that promise!

The B.C.

Brother John Hatch mentioned this at Joe's funeral (Yes, Christians can laugh, as well as cry, at funerals of believers). Brother John was on his way to speak to a group of women. He asked Joe if he had a good joke he could tell them. Joe just happened to have a printed copy of "The B.C." with him and gave it to his pastor to use. I think he used it to great effect. I later heard Brother John tell about Dad and use the B.C. story in chapel at East Texas Baptist University in Marshall, TX, on Homecoming Day in 2002. (By the way, John Hatch did not just tell this story, he also preached a great message at ETBU about Jesus being the only way to heaven.) "The B.C." follows:

My friend is a rather old-fashioned woman, always quite delicate and elegant, especially in her language. She and her husband were planning a week's vacation in Florida, so she wrote to a particular campground and asked for a reservation.

She wanted to make sure the campground was fully equipped, but didn't quite know how to ask about the toilet facilities. She just couldn't bring herself to write the word *toilet* in her letter. After much deliberation she finally decided to use the old-fashioned term *bathroom commode*. But when she wrote that down, she still felt that she was being too forward. So she started all over again, rewrote the entire letter, and referred to the bathroom commode merely as the B.C. "Does the campground have its own B.C.?" is what she finally wrote.

Well, the campground owner wasn't old-fashioned at all. When he got the letter he just couldn't figure out what the woman was talking about. That B.C. business really stumped him. After worrying about it for a while, he showed the letter to several campers, but no one could imagine what the lady meant, either. So the campground owner, finally arriving at the conclusion that the lady must be asking about the location of the Baptist church, sat down and wrote the following reply:

"Dear Madam: I regret very much the delay in answering your letter, but I now take the pleasure of informing you that a B.C. is located nine miles north of the campground and is capable of seating 250 people at one time. I admit it is quite a distance away if you are in the habit of going regularly, but no doubt you will be pleased to learn that a great number of our people take their lunches along and make a day of it. They usually arrive early and stay late. If you don't start early, you probably will not make it in time. The last time my wife and I went was six years ago, and it was so crowded we had to stand up the whole time we were there. It may interest you to know that right now, there is a supper planned to raise money to buy more seats. They're going to hold it in the basement of the B.C. I would like to say it pains me very much not being able to go more often, but it surely is not lack of desire on my part. As we grow older, it seems to be more of an effort, particularly in cold weather. If you decide to come down to our campground, perhaps I could go with you the first time you go, sit with you, and introduce you to all the other folks. Remember, this is a friendly community!"

It Didn't Work, Did It?

Joe was amused by the story told him by D. O. Foster, former pastor of FBC, Lake Jackson. Foster told of preaching at Velasco to a fine, old gentleman preacher who probably was in his early 90s. He had lost nearly all his hearing. You had to practically scream at him for him to hear.

After the worship service the old preacher asked Foster and the deacons to pray for his hearing. They were happy to do so. They gathered in a circle around the old gentleman. They bowed their heads. They began to pray aloud, one after another. When the last one had prayed, they all looked up, except the old preacher. They waited while he still had his head bowed. They waited some more.

Finally, one of the men punched him and said at full volume, "We're through now." The old preacher raised his head, looked around, and said loudly, "It didn't work, did it?"

I Knew You Were a Hard Master

Brother Joe was a regular at the UBA Monday-morning pastors conference. At one time he served as president. He also served once as treasurer. The group did not have much reason to collect money; it just met each Monday for singing, a message, and fellowship.

At the end of his year as treasurer, Joe gave his report to the president and the conference. The amount he had received was about $6.59. That is what he had at the end of the year. Joe began, "I knew that you were a hard master, reaping where you had not sown. And I was afraid, and went and hid thy $6.59 in the ground. And lo, here is thy $6.59." President Skip Smith did not miss a beat and said, "Bind that man and cast him out."

(I think Dad said that John Bisagno was at that meeting and especially had a good laugh out of that incident.)

(See Matthew 25 for the story to which they jokingly referred.)

Life Is Like

Life is like a roll of toilet paper. The closer you get to the end, the faster it goes.

I'm Ahead

In the last few years of his life Joe would say, "God has been so good to me. If He never did anything good for me again, I would be ahead."

The Nuns

Brother Joe was visiting St. Joseph's Hospital in Houston. He got on an elevator. Just before the door closed, a group of nuns entered the elevator. It now was filled with nuns and Joe Brumbelow. Noting his uncomfortable look, the head mother looked at him and said, "Blessed art thou among women."

Joe looked at her, smiled, and said, "I like you."

Biggest Industry

Brother Joe said, "I grew up in a small town. The biggest industry in Damon was the 400-pound Avon lady."

Getting Over It

Early in his ministry, Joe preached a sermon in which he demonstrated that he clearly had a great desire to see the lost come to Christ. He wanted people to be saved in that service and every time he preached. An older preacher told him, "I know you want to see people saved every time you preach. But don't worry too much about it. You will get over it. Eventually you will not be as concerned about people getting saved." Joe later prayed that God would never let him get over it.

Those who knew him best testified that he did not ever get over it. Even after he retired, he saw a numerous people saved as he served in his interim pastorates. He loved the lost right up until the day he went to be with the Lord.

It Was So Cold

Joe got this from a news clipping from the AP, originally from the Rockford Register Star, IL. The newspaper asked its readers to finish the sentence, "It was so cold that—"

• Our snowman begged us not to leave him out another night.

• Even my soft water was hard.

• We lit a candle and the flame froze before we could blow it out.

• I let my dog out, and I had to break him loose from the tree.

• Even the world leaders couldn't get into a heated argument.

- When I went out, my shadow froze to the sidewalk.
- When I called home to Arizona, the message caused the cactus to frost over.
- I baked a cake and put it outside to cool. A half-hour later, it was frosted.
- You could freeze an egg on the sidewalk.
- I saw a fish jump in the river and the splash froze.
- I had to go up and break the smoke off my chimney.
- The firemen advise you to set fire to your house.
- The altar boys had to jumpstart the candles.
- We opened the refrigerator to heat the house.
- My false teeth chattered, and they weren't even in my mouth.
- I looked out the window and saw a cottontail pushing a jackrabbit to get him started.
- When police saw a bank-robbery suspect and said, "Freeze", he did.
- The snow is turning blue.
- I put the meat in the freezer to defrost.
- I saw a 32nd-degree Mason, and he was down to 15.

Emotion vs. Faithfulness

Joe said, "It's not how high you jump; it's how straight you walk when you hit the ground."

Funeral, I Mean Wedding

One of Dad's most embarrassing moments happened in about 1960. A young man named Joe Jamison had gotten saved and baptized at Doverside Baptist Church. He had lived a rough life and even was dishonorably discharged from the military before he got saved. When the man prayed for Jesus to save him, Brother Joe remembered him saying, "God, I ain't promising you nothing. But if you can do something with me, I'm ready for you to do it." And God worked a miracle in his life. Joe Jamison even was called to preach not long after that experience.

Dad kidded with him. They had a good time together.

Joe Jamison was engaged to a young woman in the church named Bonnie Banes. This was going to make another Joe-and-Bonnie couple in the church. Everyone was talking about that. Joe and the other Joe kept kidding about the "funeral" instead of the "wedding" about to occur.

The big day arrived; Joe Brumbelow stood to speak. He said, "We are gathered here today for this funeral." He immediately corrected it, but the damage was done. Snickers could be heard all over the audience. Joe later would tell of one man he saw who quickly put his hand over his mouth to keep from laughing out loud. Joe was so seriously shaken up that he did not even show up at the reception that followed the wedding. He just went straight home.

The people knew how embarrassed he was. No one even mentioned it to him for about six months. After that, however, he was fair game and they never let him forget about the "funeral" he preached for Joe and Bonnie Jamison.

Chapter 6

The Gideon Speaker

Joe always supported the Gideons. The Gideons form an international organization of interdenominational Christian businessmen. Their goal is to distribute the Word of God—the Bible—as widely as possible. They believe in the inspiration and inerrancy of the Bible. They are the ones who put the Bibles in motels, hospitals, and prisons. Gideons distribute them, when allowed, to fifth-grade school kids. When the Gideons call on your church, allow them to visit and encourage your church to give generously to their ministry.

Joe usually had a Gideon or two as members of his church. Some worry about the Gideons draining away funds from the church. Joe never experienced that. He found the Gideons to be tithers, faithful members of their local church, and supportive of their pastor.

Gideons ask churches to allow them to address their congregations once a year. Gideons are laymen. Some are a little hesitant to speak in public. Sometimes, however, this can be a plus to their message, since the message is from a layman.

In the late 1960s when Joe was pastor of First Baptist Church, Cypress, TX, he had a member, Dick Williams, who was a Gideon. One day Williams returned home with a real story to tell his pastor. He had been asked to speak for the Gideons in a little Baptist church in the Texas Hill Country close to Johnson City. Already nervous as he sat on the platform, Williams looked toward the back of the sanctuary and saw two men walk in. The pastor asked, "Is that President Johnson?" The Gideon replied, "I don't know, but the second man is Billy Graham." Billy Graham had been visiting former President Lyndon Baines Johnson. They had decided to attend this church that Sunday. Somehow, Mr. Williams got through his message that Sunday. Afterwards, he said, both Graham and Johnson graciously commended him for his presentation.

Give Him Another Chance

Joe had a preacher friend he had known for years. Pastors don't often get to hear each other preach, since they have to be in their own pulpits each service. Joe had heard this friend preach years before. To put things mildly, the preacher had bombed out. He did a terrible job of preaching that service. For years afterward Joe, while thinking the world of his friend, realized the man just could not preach. Then Joe finally had the opportunity to hear him preach again. He dreaded attending, but it turned out to be a great service and great preaching. Joe heard him several times more. The preaching always was great.

Joe realized that for years he had incorrectly thought this guy could not preach. He knew that all preachers will bomb out from time to time. One professor said, "Remember that half of your preaching will be below average." Maybe we should give that preacher another chance.

Crooked Rows

Joe had a vegetable garden most every year, but he never could seem to get the garden rows straight. He joked, "You can grow more in a crooked row than you can a straight row."

Hospital Exercise

A preacher does difficult work, but it usually does not involve strenuous physical activity. Joe partially made up for it by taking the stairs instead of the elevator when he made hospital visits. Sometimes folks saw him breathing a little heavily. On an occasion or two a nurse wondered if he needed more help than did the patient he was visiting.

A little free medical advice: Doctors usually advise patients now to exercise continuously for about 30 minutes at least every other day. Joe began walking a couple of miles to get this kind of exercise as well.

Quakers and Baptists

Quakers do not believe in war or violence of any kind. A Quaker owned an unruly milk cow. On one occasion the cow had just kicked over the bucket full of milk. Exasperated, the Quaker said to the cow, "Thou dost know that I am a Quaker, and I cannot strike thee. But what thou dost not know is that I can sell thee to a Baptist and he shall beat the devil out of thee!"

Empty Bottles

You sometimes hear of folks who never have been born again and who switch from one denomination to another to another. Joe categorized them by saying, "I guess it doesn't matter what kind of label you put on an empty bottle."

Gardening in Bad Soil

Joe seemed to end up with the worst soil in which to garden. One location behind a parsonage (house owned by the church for its pastor to live in) was nothing but fill dirt with clay, rocks, and chunks of concrete. Some of what he learned by gardening in bad soil may help the gardeners out there:

• Gypsum helps to break up clay. Use it liberally once or twice a year. You can purchase a bag at most garden or feed stores.

• Use all the organic matter you can—leaves, compost (decomposed plant matter), mulch (bigger, less decomposed plant matter), etc. Put mulch on top of the ground when plants are two- or three-inches high. It will conserve water, suppress weeds, and add nutrients to the soil as it slowly decomposes. It also loosens clay or any type soil. (Joe also used cow, horse, chicken, or quail manure.)

• Medina, a soil activator, seemed to work miracles for him.

• When you make a furrow to plant seed, sometimes the seeds are in danger of disappearing too deep under the hard dirt and clods. (Joe would make a furrow, then fill the furrow with a store-bought bag of top soil or fine compost. He then would plant the seeds in the top soil or compost. By the time the plants were growing out of the added soil, they were big enough to handle the clay and clods. The small amount of top soil or compost helped the overall quality of the soil as well.)

• Sharp sand—sometimes called concrete sand—is about the coarsest, biggest size of sand. Use it to mix with clay or gumbo to loosen the soil and improve drainage.

• Build rows up high, or use raised beds if you have a drainage problem. Clay soil takes a long time to drain after a rain. Soil in a raised bed will remain loose if you build it narrow enough that you don't have to walk in it.

• On the positive side, clay soil holds nutrients and water well, so you don't have to fertilize and water so often.

Gold in the Hollow Tree

My uncle Bill—Joe's brother—offered the following story: When their dad, E. P. Brumbelow, was 16 (he was born in 1881), he and some others went on a hunting trip. When they woke up one morning in the woods, they made a fire in a standing hollow tree. That part of the country has enough rainfall that you don't have to worry much about forest fires.

They cooked their bacon and eggs over the fire in the open hollow tree. The fire began to roar up into the hollow. They noticed that some molten bits of metal began to drop out of the tree and into the frying pan. They did not think much about it except that they were upset that it ruined their breakfast. They left the fire burning and went on with their hunting.

Some time later, as the story goes, a man from the area in which they had been hunting showed up in town with a large hunk of metal that obviously had been burned. It was tested and

proved to be gold. The man took it with him and never was
heard from again.

The story continues that several years before the hunting trip
a stagecoach had been robbed in the area and the money never
recovered. Could it be . . .?

I can't personally vouch for the above, but it does make a
fascinating story.

Spitting Over Your Chin
An old man said, "Before I started taking Hadacol, I couldn't
spit over my chin. Now I can spit all over my chin!"

Motto
Early in Joe's ministry he often used as a motto for church
letterheads and other items, "Preaching the Bible, the Blood, and
the Blessed Hope."

Decent Swim Suits?
The last decent swim suit I saw had a hole in the elbow!

How About a Coke®?
While in college, Joe wondered if the professors really read
all his papers that he turned in. So halfway into one research
paper, in the middle of a paragraph, he wrote, "If you read this
far, I'll buy you a Coke®." He got a good grade for the paper but
never was asked to produce the money for a Coke®.

Taking his lead, I once tried the same thing in college. I
never heard a word about it from the professor.

Bad Food at UCC
Before he married, Joe lived in the single dorms at the
University of Corpus Christi (UCC). They were old military bar-
racks with community restrooms. The restrooms did not leave
much to privacy or modesty. They merely had a long line of
commodes.

One day UCC must have gotten a bad batch of food in the cafeteria. About one or two in the morning Joe got terribly sick. He rushed down the hallway to the restroom. He opened the door in the wee hours of the morning and looked at the long line of commodes. Every seat was taken!

"My Toe's On Fire!"

During World War II a blackout of lights faced the Gulf of Mexico. German submarines had been in the Gulf. You could camp on the beach, but before dark, the campfire had to be extinguished or shielded from the Gulf. You could flounder, but the lantern light had to be shaded on the Gulf side. Coast Guard men patrolled the beach and passed your camp in the night.

During this time, on an overnight fishing trip at Surfside, the Brumbelow clan was camped on the beach. As a kid, Joe's brother, Bill, had a problem of walking in his sleep. Their dad was sincerely concerned that Bill might walk in his sleep and walk right into the Gulf. So they tied a rope around his ankle and tied the other end to something in camp.

In the middle of the night they were awakened by Bill's screams. He had jumped up yelling, "My toe's on fire, my toe's on fire!" Bill ran until he got to the end of his rope. The rope jerked him down. He was lying spread-eagle on the ground still saying, "My toe's on fire."

They thought he was just having a bad dream until they checked his blanket. Sure enough, where Bill's toe had been was a hole burned into the blanket. An ember from the campfire flipped over onto Bill's blanket during the night. I think a Coast Guard Patrol had just passed by. No one ever learned whether the Coast Guard entered this incident into its official report.

Speaking of Toes

Once or twice Joe was with one of his grandchildren when he or she stubbed a toe. Like the rest of us would do at such a time, the grandchild would whimper and look for sympathy.

Their granddad (usually called Papaw) would look greatly concerned and say, "Do you think we ought to call the tow truck?"

Living What You Preach with Grandkids

Joe had preached through the years about the importance of missions and the Lord's work. If your son or daughter gets called to the mission field, be proud. Don't hold that child back. He would tell about some parents that were for missions until their child surrendered to the ministry. Then they would say, "Not my child. They'll never make any money. It's dangerous. It's too far away." Or, "They're not taking my grandchildren that far away."

Brother Joe's oldest son, Steve, was in evangelism. He was preaching a revival in an American Baptist church in West Virginia when a pastorless Southern Baptist church in the area visited to hear him. He was not interested, but the church persisted. More importantly, God persisted. Steve was called to Cross Lanes Baptist Church in Cross Lanes, WV, and had a great ministry there for just over 14 years.

When Steve and Nelda were called, they had two children, Amy (2 1/2) and Lori, (2 months). Bonnie took care of the girls while the parents went in view of a call. Here they were, about to take Joe and Bonnie's only two grandchildren 1,000 miles away.

Joe and Bonnie determined that they were going to live what they had preached and taught through the years. Though it was one of their greatest sacrifices, Joe and Bonnie gave their blessing as Steve and his family went to West Virginia.

Rat Now

Joe sometimes enjoyed acting less educated than he was. He told about the school teacher who asked a boy in her class to spell rat. The boy stood up and said, "R-A-T." "No, no," the teacher replied. "I mean like 'rat' now."

Joe joked that he was grown before he knew that *wash* did not have an "r" in it. He was so poor, he was grown before he knew an apple had a core or that a watermelon had a rind!

Joe quipped that Bonnie was so country that when they married, she tried to blow out the light bulb on their wedding night.

Humor That Can't Be Corrected

Sometimes what is meant to be harmless humor can't be straightened out later.

In 1981 Joe and his family attended the Southern Baptist annual convention in Los Angeles. Having protesters of all kinds at the SBC is common. That year was no exception. One young man in particular was just outside the convention hall ranting and raving about how evil the SBC was. A small crowd of Baptists had gathered to hear a few of his accusations. One Baptist messenger in the crowd turned to Joe and said, "That fellow is some kind of nut." Joe could not resist and replied, "That's my youth director." Joe's director of missions, Bob Fraiser, heard the whole thing and started laughing.

Joe then turned around to tell the messenger that he was only kidding. The messenger was long gone. In case that Baptist messenger is reading this book, Joe was only joking.

Poetry I Thought Dad Must Have Written

Growing up I heard Dad quote some lines of poetry. I mistakenly thought he must have written them!

Mom knew this one and taught it to Dad just after they had gotten married:

> "They walked down the dusty road,
> The sky ablaze with stars,
> And when they came to the rusty gate
> He let down the rusty bars.
> She passed and did not thank him,
> She seemed to know not how,
> For he was just a farmer boy,
> And she a jersey cow."

Others:

"A boy stood on a burning deck,
His feet were filled with blisters.
His pants and shirt were burned,
So he had to wear his sister's."

"In Fourteen hundred and ninety-two,
Columbus sailed the ocean blue.
He sailed so slow he stumped his toe,
In fourteen hundred and ninety-two."

"Kiss me quick and let me go,
Here comes Papa with a grubbing hoe."

OK, maybe some other literary giant wrote them, but Dad's still my hero!

Joe under the Desk

Charlene Barnes Johnson, who grew up in Damon, tells of Joe getting in trouble with the first-grade teacher. The teacher put little Joe under her desk. Every time he moved she kicked him.

I wonder what the authorities would say about that today? Fortunately, it did not seem to stunt his psyche too badly.

Halloween and Outhouses

Back in the old days Damon is said to have gone a little wild at Halloween. One of the ingrained practices: kids roaming the town and turning over outhouses. Joe's stepmother (his mom died when he was 6; his dad later married Wadie) was in a real dilemma one Halloween evening. She needed to use the facilities but realized the danger on Halloween. Finally, with a look of resolve on her face, she went out back. A few moments after the outhouse door closed, her worst fears were realized. She heard the rustling of feet. The walls of the outhouse begin to shake.

Thinking that not even boys in Damon would think of overturning an occupied outhouse, she called out. "Boys, if you'll just let me finish, I'll help you turn over the outhouse!"

She was pleased that the outhouse was not turned over. She was not pleased to find that the culprit was her own, dear husband. Maybe practical joking just runs in the family.

Y2K Panic

You may remember the Y2K panic. The fear was that computers were not originally designed to properly turn over to the year 2000. When the new year occurred, speculation was that computers would switch to 00 or 1900, disintegrate, and life would end as we know it. Joe enjoyed a joke related to this, but a person had to be a certain age to understand it. He announced in 1999 that all families needed to check their toilet paper to make sure that it was Y2K-compatible. If not, at midnight of the new year it would turn back into Sears catalogs!

For the younger folks who never knew the good old days: Toilet paper was difficult to find. Popular substitutes in outhouses were Sears catalogs, corn cobs, etc.

Fruit Trees Joe Grew

When he had the chance, Joe grew a vegetable garden. In his later years he planted more fruit trees. Some of the ones he planted, and ones that do well in the upper Gulf Coast region of Texas (USDA Zone 9):

• Citrus trees: Miewa Kumquat, Bell Tangerine, Pong Koa Mandarin.

In this area if citrus is not growing on its own roots, it should be grafted onto trifoliate (poncirus trifoliata or a variation called Flying Dragon) rootstock. Uncle Bill helped us find a source of trifoliates growing wild. We put several in pots and in 2002 we grafted the Pong Koa onto a trifoliate. (The above citrus, if healthy and well-watered, do not need protection unless the temperature drops below 22 degrees Fahrenheit.)

• Pear: Orient, Pineapple. A newer, better fresh-eating pear is Tennessee. Joe grafted a Tennessee scion onto one of his trees.

• Peach: Tropic Snow, Tropic Sweet; previously mentioned.

• Pecan: Caddo. Good pecans for the eastern half of Texas include Caddo, Kanza, Desirable, Prilop, Cheyenne, and native pecans from your area.

• Pomegranate: Eve.

• Fig: Osborne Prolific. LSU Purple is also a good variety for the area.

• Persimmon: Eureka, Fuyu. Fuyu is a persimmon that is not astringent; you can eat it while it is still firm. Most are astringent; they have to be fully ripe and soft, or else.

Joe told about the kid that slipped persimmon juice into the grape juice for the Lord's Supper. At the conclusion of the service the preacher stood and said, "We will now rise and whistle the benediction."

(Never plant a tree deeper than it originally was growing. Plant in a sunny, well-drained area. Spread out the roots as you backfill with the same dirt that came out of the hole. Do not leave roots in a circle in the hole; spread them out like spokes on a wheel. Water well. Use mulch and protect from weed-eaters.)

Tomatoes

• Joe usually planted tomatoes about the first part of March. Plant them early so they can be producing before the hottest part of summer. They probably will need some protection from the cold. Joe was known to lose them in a freeze and have to plant again. He would plant tomatoes deeper than they originally were growing (don't do that with peppers, trees, or most any other plant) in full sun. Water well after transplanting. It also helps to plant tomatoes in a different area (rotate) each year.

• Favorite tomato stakes—steel T-Posts used for barbed-wire (in Texas often pronounced *Bob-Wire*) fences. Six or eight feet long. Drive them in the ground with a T-Post Driver. Will just about last forever.

• Tomato cages—livestock panels. They are made in a 16-foot panel. Cut them in half with bolt cutters; bend each in a circle. They make two durable, long-lasting cages. You also can make them from three short pieces of livestock panel to form a triangle. Then they can be folded for storage.

• Tomato ties—1/4-inch-wide green vinyl tape available at nurseries.

• Types of tomatoes—Joe grew Juliet, Sweet 100, Yellow Pear, Celebrity, Porter, Porter Improved, etc. Another good but difficult-to-find tomato is Sweet Chelsea.

Joe said that when he was young, people bought tomatoes differently. Sellers would have bunches of tomato transplants growing together. You told them how many you wanted. The seller would just pull them up out of the dirt. They then were wrapped in wet newspapers. You hurried home to get them in the ground. The seller usually gave you a few extras. You expected some to not make it.

Bonnie Brumbelow grows all types of flowers. Some of her favorite antique-type roses include Maggie, China Doll, Cadenza, and Duchess de Brabant. She also has butterfly and hummingbird attractors like Hamelia, Cuphea (David Verity), Tithonia, Lantana, and Butterfly Weed.

Faith?

God wants us to have faith, but He also wants us to use our brains. Be willing to listen to the advice of others. Proverbs 11:14 tells us that in the multitude of counselors is safety.

When some Christian was getting a little too far out on a limb, Joe sometimes pointed out, "There's a thin line between faith and ignorance."

That's Too Spiritual

The Bible is clear that sex before or outside of marriage is wrong in God's eyes. But God created sex for procreation and the enjoyment and fulfillment of married couples. Joe also believed the biblical teaching that marriage is to be between one man and one woman. Contrary to the opinion of some today, Jesus did directly speak to the gay-marriage issue when He said, "A man (singular, male) shall leave his father and mother and be joined to his wife (singular, female)" (Mark 10:7). Joe referred to Hebrews 13:4 (KJV), "Marriage is honourable in all, and the bed undefiled" in explaining that sex in marriage is right and proper.

A preacher once met with Joe and some other preachers. The preacher shared his deeper life experience. He said he had gotten so spiritual that he hadn't touched his wife in six months. Joe later said he prayed, "Lord, don't let me get that spiritual!"

Expositors of the Bible

Some of Joe's favorite Bible expositors (commentaries, sermon books, etc.) included: H. A. Ironside, John Phillips, W. A. Criswell, Warren Weirsbe, J. Vernon McGee, Hershel Ford, John R. Rice, Adrian Rogers, Clovis Chappell, Clarence McCartney, W. E. Munsey, R. L. Sumner, Tom Malone (Joe visited and witnessed to Malone's dad, who lived on Apache Street on the north side of Houston. Malone later told me that his dad had gotten saved in his later years.), Hyman Appleman, D. L. Moody, R. A. Torrey, R. G. Lee, Charles Allen, R. Earl Allen, George W. Truett, E. J. Daniels, Jerry Vines, Walter B. Knight, Vance Havner, Alexander Maclaren, John MacArthur, C. H. Spurgeon, Billy Sunday, Gypsy Smith, B. H. Carroll, and L. R. Scarborough.

As I grew up, I remember seeing many of these authors' books on the bookshelves at home and in Dad's office. Joe did not agree with every author on every point, but these are many of the books and authors he used. (When I started preaching at age 13, Dad told me that Moody Press, Bible book publisher from the days of D. L. Moody, could be trusted. "I've never gotten a book from them that was doctrinally unsound," he said.)

The Girl Who Saved His Ministry

All pastors have bad days. Things can get mighty lonely and discouraging. Sometimes Mondays are the worst. One Monday morning early in Joe's ministry he decided he could not take it any longer. He got a sheet of church stationary out of his desk drawer and wrote out his resignation as pastor. He was absolutely sincere. He was not going to put up with things as they were any longer. He folded it and put it back in the desk drawer. He would read it to the church the next Wednesday night.

Feeling pretty low, he went to his car and began driving around the community. He drove down Berry Road, then back to the church. He drove behind the church where Duff Lane ended in the back church-parking lot. As he drove slowly down Duff Lane, he saw a group of girls playing in one of the yards. He heard one little girl call to him, "Brother Joe, please stop." After he stopped, the little girl ran to the car and said, "Hi, Brother Joe, how are you today?" He answered, "Fine" but later confessed that he lied! Then the little girl said, "I wanted my friends to meet you. I've been telling them how you told me about Jesus and I got saved and then how you 'baba-tized' me. Brother Joe, thank you for telling me about Jesus. Thank you for 'baba-tizing' me." She then introduced her friends each by name. They all went back to their playing.

Joe returned to his office, took out his letter of resignation, and tore it into little bits. He later said, "No one could have gotten me to leave for anything. That little girl did not realize it, but she may have saved my ministry." God began to work there as never before. The next year more than 100 were baptized at Doverside Baptist Church.

Chapter 7

The Preacher's Wife

I asked Mom to write something, based on her experience, to young preachers' wives. Then I gave her the whole chapter. Her comments follow:

I Married the Preacher

Just imagine a young 20-year-old pastor with a 17-year-old wife making their best effort to lead a church. How patient and longsuffering those dear people must have been! Joe had pastors, preacher friends, and professors who were such an encouragement. I had much respect and admiration for some dear pastors' wives that I knew. Mrs. C. C. Larrison, whose husband had been pastor of First Baptist Church of Old Ocean where I grew up, and Mrs. Lowe, whose husband had been my pastor after I moved to First Baptist Church of Rosenberg, both were quiet, sweet women with an impressive spirit about them. Then, a few years after we were married, I met another pastor's wife that I probably learned from more than anyone. This was Mrs. Harvey Graham, whose husband was pastor of the Calvary Baptist Church in Corpus Christi, TX. She labored so unselfishly beside her husband, took care of a family of five girls, and was the most effective Bible teacher I had met. All three of these ladies have been in heaven for a number of years. Someday I intend to tell them how their lives impressed me.

As the years passed, Joe and I were experiencing almost every conceivable situation known to anyone. After 51 years of being a preacher's wife, I realize some things were so very important and helped me so much.

1. BE YOUR HUSBAND'S BEST FAN AND SUPPORTER AND BEST FRIEND! Let him know he can depend on you. Try to make a home life that is special and a safe haven to which your family will be happy to return. Don't be critical, picky, always finding fault in things he does (a few church members will take care of that). Remember, he is the only pastor you have, so take good care of him!

2. DO TAKE YOUR POSITION SERIOUSLY! You are an example. Every Christian, whether a pastor's wife or not, should take that position seriously. At the same time, be friendly and pleasant. Be genuine; be yourself.

3. BE KIND TO THE UNLOVELY AS WELL AS THE LOVELY! You will have to identify with poor, unlearned, intelligent, affluent, sweet, mean, pretty, and ugly. If you have a difficult time loving people no matter what their status in life, pray much about it. Except for God's grace you could be in the same circumstances as those with whom you will work.

4. LEARN WHEN TO TALK AND WHEN NOT TO! People will approach you with all kinds of church, family, and personal problems. Let them be able to talk with you and have the assurance that you will not spread all the news. DO NOT SHARE PERSONAL THINGS ABOUT YOUR FAMILY! Keep personal opinions to yourself and your husband.

5. BE A GOOD LISTENER! People need someone who will listen to them—to be able to get their problems off their chest. Many times you may be able to give good advice that will be helpful. Pray with those who approach you for counsel.

6. BE A GOOD BIBLE STUDENT! Realize that God's Word is a lamp and light. You need wisdom that is derived only through study.

7. HAVE SPECIAL FAMILY TIME INCLUDING BIBLE READING AND PRAYER! Joe always said, "No matter how good a job I do at the church, if I fail my family, I'm a failure." That's a good thing for wives to remember, also.

8. DO NOT FEEL EXEMPT FROM ACCEPTING RESPONSIBILITIES IN CHURCH WORK! Do your share. However, some church activities are just not your thing. Don't commit to things with which you cannot deal. I found some people can just plain do a better job than I can at some activities of the church.

9. TRY TO HAVE SOME KIND OF DIVERSION, HOBBY, ETC.! I have too much. I have a room of undone hobbies. Really, some special interest is good for you.

10. AVOID SHOWING FAVORITES IN THE CHURCH FAMILY! You always will be closer to some people, but be careful how you deal with it. Try to make everyone feel special!

11. IF YOU CAN'T COOK, LEARN TO! Perfect a few specialties. They don't have to be gourmet (unless you choose to do so); just good, simple food will do. No doubt, a time will arise when you simply must entertain, so be prepared. I have known some who are really good at their specialty and claim that is all they can do, but that is sufficient.

12. SEIZE THE MOMENT AND SAVOR THE TASTE! Being a preacher's wife is a special office to fill. God has called you to do it. The rewards are so much greater than are all of the work, disappointments, failures, and problems. I cannot imagine any other lifestyle being so fulfilling and wonderful.

Thank You, Father, for permitting me to have this place that you gave to me.

Living with the Preacher

Joe and I always liked a song Country singer Charlie Pride made popular years ago. It started like this:

> "Seems like only yesterday we fell in love,
>   Just barely old enough to be sincere.
> Back then I thought I loved you all I could,
> But I've grown to love you more through the years."

We were just barely old enough to be sincere, but we were sincere! I probably never would have believed it if someone had suggested that someday I would marry a preacher. I still cannot understand why God saw fit to choose me for the place He did, but I thank Him for doing so. When Joe visited First Baptist Church of Old Ocean, TX to preach in the absence of our pastor, I had a strange feeling that this would be a lasting relationship. He had brought with him Roy Cloudt from Damon. I had known Roy at West Columbia High School the previous year. When they entered the building and sat down in the back before Sunday School, Roy pointed out my sister, Stella, to him and told Joe she had been in his graduating class. Joe later told me he replied, "But I'm interested in that one sitting next to her." I was the one sitting next to her. Our pastor was gone in view of a call to another church that day. In the process of his moving Joe was supply pastor at our church several times that summer. He was home for the summer break from the University of Corpus Christi. Things became more and more interesting. When he had to return to college, we corresponded very much. The following spring he proposed to me while we were sitting in the car in front of the old Hagemeier Grocery Store in West Columbia. When I graduated from West Columbia High School in May, 1950, he gave me a Bible. The store salesman asked if he wanted to have my name imprinted on the front. Joe told them to imprint just the name "Bonnie." When questioned further about the last name, Joe replied, "I intend to change that as soon as possible."

Many things were so impressive to me about Joe: His love and commitment to the Lord; his concern for others, especially those in need of a Savior, his capacity to love people no matter their status in life; and the feeling that he was so real (he never could have put on an act if he wanted to). He was a perfect gentleman and had deep Christian convictions. Of course, there was this sense of humor! Some of the first things he discussed with me were his salvation experience and his call to preach. He knew God had called him to preach!

We were married April 7, 1951. By that time he was pastor of a small church and later would return to his school work. God truly gave us a marriage that I never could have imagined—a closeness I cannot describe, a dependence on each other that was so warm and heartfelt. We never grew tired of each other, but instead the love, admiration, and respect grew like the years. We served the Lord together, visited together, prayed together, cried together, laughed together, reared our children together. Life for us was a "together" thing. One lady told me, "You two are like Siamese twins."

We had so many experiences to go through. The first time he took me fishing, I never had seen anything like it. We went down to the San Bernard River close to Damon and set out throw lines. He told me we would come back to check them. Late that night when we began driving into those dark woods, I couldn't believe it. You could not see your hand in front of your face because of the darkness. Thank God for flashlights! He had a big, blue catfish on one of the lines, so I guess it was worth it. Joe surely thought so; he loved fishing!

The first big rain we had after we married was an experience. The house we lived in was old and worn. We began to hear water dripping. That night we ended up having to use all our pots and pans to put under drips. The landlord did repair it, though.

When I learned of all the school episodes he had been involved in at Damon, that also was an experience. This man had a reputation! I once told him if I had known him in school, I probably would not have taken a second look at him. That may be why God did not let us meet sooner. This humor thing of his did get him in trouble in school from time to time.

Our first real disappointment we faced was in September, 1952, when our little girl was stillborn after an eight-month pregnancy. We later had our three healthy sons: Joe Stephen, David Randall, and Ronald Mark. I was outnumbered in our family!

During those early years in the pastorate we did just about everything. Joe would have all the deacon meetings, committee

113

meetings, building committees, finance committees, and any others you could think of besides regular things such as visits, phone calls, hospital visits (that was an all-day task before the freeway system was built in Houston), office work, studying much, etc. He always was a diligent worker at whatever he became involved in and was a good pastor. For a number of years I did the secretarial work for the church. Since I had small children at home, I did it at home. I never will forget the old-time mimeograph machines (stencils had to be cut on a typewriter or cut with a stylus). When you finished running all your copies, you were just about as black as the ink you were using. Church bulletins, church directories, and most Vacation Bible School materials were done on the mimeograph. The typewriters were not electric, either.

We enjoyed our work. Joe always felt such a responsibility toward his church and loved his people dearly. During the 1950s and 1960s I believe people were more responsive. We had some wonderful revivals through the years. We might have many, many baptisms every year. I am amazed at how God poured out His richest blessings, even when heartbreaks and disappointments occurred, plans had to be changed, promises were postponed, and even vacations were canceled because of church emergencies. One of the difficult times was moving from one church to another. You know and are assured of God's leading, but it just breaks your heart to leave the dear people you have worked with and loved so much, knowing you will never again see many of them here on earth. Every time I read the Apostle Paul's letters and feel the tenderness and love he expressed, I think I know some of the special ways he felt.

We thoroughly enjoyed our family, perhaps because Joe and I were growing up with them. Every time I see a little blond-haired boy, I'm reminded of days gone by. All of our boys are different, but they all have some of the same characteristics. They all love the Lord. I thank God for that. They are all diligent workers. They all inherited their Dad's sense of humor and his love for fishing and hunting. At our home, we had times, such as Thanksgiving dinner, that we had to plan according to the hunting schedule. I even put off cataract surgery a few years ago until deer season was over!

Most preachers do not make an impressive salary. When the boys all were fairly young, Joe and I wanted to do something special for them. They got to go hunting and fishing occasionally, but we thought they needed a special treat. We saved for several months and finally felt as though we could afford to take them to Six Flags (then only in the Dallas-Fort Worth area). We did not tell them ahead of time and thought a surprise would be good.

When Joe called them all in one evening and told them what we were going to do the next day, a disappointing chorus sounded: "But Daddy, we wanted to go rabbit hunting." Laying aside our original plans and realizing how strong these inherited traits were, we rose early the next morning and headed for Damon and let them make the tracks that some other Brumbelow boys had made years earlier. Our trip ended up a lot cheaper than we had expected!

Humor emerged in just about everything. At times when the boys were younger, we thought they might kill each other before they ever grew up. They get along a lot better since they don't live in the same house and actually enjoy being together!

When the grandchildren started arriving, we were excited. Stephen and his wife, Nelda, had Amy first and then Lori two years later. Their favorite time at our house was for Papaw to play bear with them. He would wait until they were in bed at night and then very quietly crawl (really) down the hallway and slip up on them and growl like a bear. Of course, their screams could be heard for a city block, but they loved it.

When Mark and Cherry married and had the grandsons— Daniel Wayne, Micah Joseph, and Jeremiah—Joe had arthritis in his back so bad he couldn't crawl around on the floor. (He had to play bear standing up.)

Joe loved to eat. It showed! He wanted to taste everything I cooked. His reasoning was, "You can't feed someone something that isn't good!" In 1987, he found that he was a diabetic. This was a tragedy for him! He loved sweets. He later said the stock in Little Debbie Cake Rolls and Butterfinger candy bars hit bottom when he quit buying them. (You will find a few of his favorite recipes in Appendix 1.)

Joe always was close to his dad. His mother had died when he was 6 years old. His memories of her were rather limited. In 1975, at the age of 93, Grandpa (Bud Brumbelow) went home to be with the Lord. Joe was in the hospital. He had been having a lot of problems. After much testing they found he was going to have to schedule gallbladder surgery but not until they could get a stomach ulcer healed. The nurse called me at work about Joe's Dad. I immediately called Dr. Homer Taylor and asked if he thought Joe could get out of the hospital. He told me to leave for Memorial Downtown Hospital and he would have him released when I arrived. This happened on Friday; we had to go to Rosenberg to make funeral arrangements. I knew Joe was very sick; I was really concerned about him. The rest of his family agreed that Sunday afternoon 2 p.m. would be a good time for the funeral services to be held at Damon Baptist Church. We lived on the north side of Houston, which was quite a drive from Damon. Some of the deacons at Doverside told Joe they would take care of a supply for Sunday, but he told them he had it covered. Then he told me he was going to preach Sunday morning and I discouraged it. I will never forget what he told me. He explained that this would be the first time his mother and daddy together ever have had the opportunity to hear him preach and "I WILL PREACH SUNDAY MORNING." I definitely believe our Father permitted them to do just that. Even though we had a long drive after church, we did make it to the funeral on time.

In 1992 Joe retired from the full-time pastorate. He immediately became an interim pastor and served five churches in that capacity. We enjoyed that work and met some dear people in those churches. When he was not doing interims, he did supply preaching a lot. We had joined First Baptist Church in Lake Jackson, TX, but were not able to attend there much because of his preaching. For the first time in our lives we were mailing our tithe to the church. He was excited in having a pastor of his own. He commented he had not had one in well over 40 years. In February, 1998, Brother John Hatch, our pastor of First Baptist Church, asked Joe to join the staff as minister of pastoral care. He did; it proved to be some of his happiest years in the ministry. He always said he never wanted to just be laid on the shelf in his older years but wanted to finish the race well. I really enjoyed getting to sit by him in church. I had never had that privilege before.

During these years of semi-retirement he was asked to speak several times about his years in the ministry. He liked to refer to the song that Howard Goodman wrote (used here by permission of Goodman Ministries, *www.Goodmanministries.com*)

"I don't regret a mile I've traveled for my Lord,
I don't regret the times I've trusted in His Word.
I have seen the years go by, many days without a song,
But I don't regret a mile I've traveled for my Lord.

I've dreamed many a dream that never came true
And I've seen them vanish at dawn,
But enough of my dreams have come true
To make me keep dreaming on.

I've prayed many a prayer and seemed no answer
would come,
Though I've waited patient and long.
But enough answers have come to those prayers
To make me keep praying on.

I've sown many a seed that's fell by the wayside
For the birds to feed upon.

But I've held enough golden sheaves in my hand
To make me keep sowing on.

I've trusted many a friend that failed me
And left me to weep alone,
But enough of my friends have been true blue
To make me keep trusting on.

Sometimes it seems that I've drawn the cup
of disappointment and pain
And gone many a day without a song,
But I've sipped enough nectar from the roses of life
To make me want to live on.

I don't regret a mile I've traveled for my Lord,
I don't regret the times I've trusted in His Word.
I have seen the years go by, many days without a song.
But I don't regret a mile I've traveled for my Lord."

Many days were without a song during these times I have talked about, but the joys and rewards so outweighed those times. It almost seemed like our Father was saving some of the very best until the last. We had some preacher friends who retired and ended up being rather critical of their pastors (they felt they could have done a better job of it). We were so thankful for the pastor God gave to us. Joe had nothing but praise for Brother Hatch. Joe loved and admired him so much. Our home church was so loving and supportive of Joe as he worked here in Lake Jackson. People still remark concerning their love and care for him.

One thing Joe regretted all his life was that he COULD NOT sing. In fact, he was tone-deaf. Oh, he would sing but could not carry a tune to anything. When the boys were small, he would sing "Jesus Loves Me," and they would say, "Daddy, that's not right." He had told Brother Harvey Graham about this when he arrived to preach in a revival for us. Brother Graham had been a music teacher when the Lord called him to preach and was a fabulous singer. He could sing "Old-Fashioned Meeting" and "God Leads His Dear Children Along" better than anyone. Brother Graham replied no one existed who could not carry a tune. The first night of the revival services they were sitting side by side during the song service when Brother Graham leaned over and said, "You sure can't, can you?" When we were traveling together, we would sing "You Are My Sunshine" and "Let Us Have a Little Talk With Jesus." You should have heard it! We would have to stop because of our laughter—it was unbelievable. I would not trade the memories we made together in 51 years for the whole world.

Heaven was so real to Joe. He always told me, "When I'm gone, I won't be dead. I'll be more alive than I've ever been before." That belief was contagious. I can't help but believe he's just in the room up higher. He even gave me so many instructions about what he wanted and did not want me doing after he was gone. It's almost like he knew he would be leaving soon.

Life isn't the same anymore since God called Joe home. I miss him terribly—I have no way to describe it. Except for God's faithfulness, His constant presence, strength and comfort, my family, my dear church family, and friends, I surely would not have the strength to go on. I look so forward to seeing him again. When I reach heaven, I think one of the first things Jesus will let me hear is that precious, familiar voice that even may be harmonizing beautifully with the sweet psalmist of Israel—David himself. Even the angels will stop to listen! I then want to kneel hand in hand with Joe and together praise our Father for letting us have a small part in His work here on earth. I want to thank Him also for just letting me be Mrs. Joe E. Brumbelow.

Thank You, dear Father, for your faithfulness through the years as we tried to serve you, in spite of our weaknesses and failures. Thank You that you do lead your dear children along!
—Mrs. Joe E. (Bonnie) Brumbelow

Chapter 8

Trapping

Grandpa (E. P. Brumbelow) did some trapping back in the old days. I have trapped off and on beginning when I was in college. While some oppose trapping, interestingly, trapping can help balance nature. For example, a study in the late 1990s showed that waterfowl more than doubled their nesting success when trapping was permitted in their nesting area. Why? Because furbearers such as fox, raccoons, and bobcats eat eggs and baby birds. On at least one occasion a birding society opposed a law that would ban trapping, because it knew if trapping were banned, it would mean a sharp decline in the bird population. Trapping uses a wildlife resource, balances and enhances nature, brings income to the state instead of costing it, gets a person closer to nature, and puts us in touch with how many of our ancestors made a living.

In recent years an upturn in cougars and other large predators attacking humans has occurred. This is something that once was unheard of. In most of those cases, the attacks occurred in states that do not allow hunting and trapping of those animals. The animals learn that they have nothing to fear from human beings. They begin to see humans simply as another kind of prey. If hunting and trapping were allowed, licensing fees would bring revenue to the state. The animals most threatening to humans would be controlled. The biggest, boldest cougar that is the least afraid of humans is the first one that is going to be shot. Hunting and trapping also have limits so that the overall animal population is not threatened. Some people are troubled that hunting is cruel; it is not nearly so cruel as nature itself, in which predators eat their prey alive or animals die difficult deaths from disease and starvation. Dads—take your kids hunting, fishing, and help them to understand and enjoy God's great outdoors.

While in Dawson I did some trapping and also ordered a couple of snares. Dad laughed at the flimsy looking snare and said, "I'll eat anything you catch in that thing, guts and all." Not long after, I caught a skunk in the snare. Dad was a man of integrity, but that was one occasion in which he refused to keep his word.

Annuity Board

For years in his ministry, Joe sent the standard $33.33 monthly retirement amount to the Annuity Board (now GuideStone Financial Resources of the SBC). The Annuity Board is an agency of the SBC. It invests retirement funds sent in by pastors or by their churches. Some churches give to the Annuity Board for their staffs; most smaller churches do not. So if anything is sent, it is sent by the pastor from his own salary. If the pastor does not send anything in, of course, he will not have any funds for retirement. Joe had many preacher friends who did not, or could not, set aside anything for retirement. He saw them struggle financially in their later years. (You or your church can contribute to a special fund set up by GuideStone to assist needy retired pastors or their widows. See Appendix 1.)

Later in his ministry Joe realized that $33.33 was not nearly enough. He began to increase his retirement savings. Joe and Bonnie did not end up with a lot, but they did end up with more than many preachers do.

On retirement Joe chose an option in which, on his death, allowed Bonnie to continue to receive the entire amount (rather than that amount being cut in half). He was proud of doing so. His own monthly annuity income was a little lower because of his decision, but his chief concern was for his wife.

The Annuity Board was very helpful during the time after Joe's death. Joe would want to tell young preachers today to make the sacrifice and plan something for retirement. If your church does not send something in, take it out of your own salary. Have the church send it in for you. If you never see the money, you won't miss it. If you contribute, the state convention also will contribute a small monthly amount to your retirement and also a disability and death benefit. Preachers: make wise use of your money. Laypeople: ask if your church is able to contribute something to GuideStone for your pastor and staff members' retirement. A little contributed in their early years can go a long way.

Honey, Let Me Take It for a Spin

Joe was a diligent worker and enjoyed yard work. He also believed his job, and not Bonnie's, was to mow the yard. He didn't think a woman would look right mowing the yard when the house had an able-bodied man in it. In Dawson, TX, the parsonage was right on the main drag through town. On a hot summer day Joe was mowing the front yard. He was sweaty, hot, and tired. Bonnie brought him a big glass of iced tea. He sat down under a live oak tree to drink it. Bonnie said, "Let me mow a little, while you drink your tea." There was Brother Joe, sitting under a tree drinking a glass of tea while Bonnie was pushing the lawn mower. Joe said that during those few moments every deacon and half his church members drove by.

Of Buzzards and Christians

Joe preached about those Christians who, even though they have so much for which to be thankful, always are critical.

He noted that the buzzard (or vulture) flies over beautiful meadows, hills, and streams and never notices them. It flies over fields of grain, green pastures, wild flowers, and great forests. But the buzzard pays no attention. What gets his attention? In the midst of a world of beauty, he zeroes in on a stinking, rotting carcass of an animal somewhere. That is all he notices. That is all he cares about.

Some Christians are like that.

Good Buddy, Please Help Me; I'm Burning

Joe was pastor of Doverside Baptist Church on the north side of Houston in the late 1950s. During that time work was begun on Interstate 45 North from Houston to Dallas. A part of that freeway would run close to the area where he served as pastor.

A woman that was loved by everyone in the church was affectionately called Mama Jones. She was very poor and very sick with cancer. She lived in Kashmere Gardens. Kashmere Gardens Baptist Church had relocated; Doverside was not that far away. Some of the Doverside members would give her a ride to church when she was able to attend.

Mama Jones was concerned about her son. She called him her prodigal son. He returned home and was living with her. He got a job driving some heavy road equipment on this new freeway.

On one occasion Joe went to see Mama Jones' son. He looked like he had not slept in days. Brother Joe asked what was wrong. He told the following story.

Traffic was bad with the construction going on. A new white car, driven by a nice-looking young woman, was in the line of traffic between two large trailer trucks. In the construction, she had to stop quickly behind traffic. The truck behind her could not stop in time. It ran into the back of her car, crushing it between the two trucks. Mr. Jones saw the wreck and jumped off his equipment to run help. He saw the driver of the first truck was OK; then he saw the woman had been crushed to death. He could do nothing to help her. He then went to the back truck. The driver said, "I'm OK, but my foot is caught. If you could help me get it loose, I'd appreciate it." His foot and leg were pinned in tightly; they could not free it. Then the gas tank of the white car burst into flames. The flames began to reach into the second truck where the man's leg and foot were pinned. The heat and then the flames began to reach the pinned truck driver. "Good buddy," the trucker called to Mr. Jones, "please help me. I'm burning. Good buddy, please help me, I'm burning, I'm burning."

Mr. Jones said, "Brother Joe, I hear those words night and day. I try to sleep, but all I can hear is that man begging me to help him out. I had to stand there and watch him burn. It's about to drive me crazy. I tried my best, but I couldn't help him." He then said, "Brother Joe, if hell is anything like that, I don't want anything to do with it."

People all around us are going to hell—a place of eternal fire and torment. Believers in Christ have the answer. May we do all within our power to save another lost soul from hell. The same Bible that tells of the glories of heaven also tells of the horrors of hell. Jesus spoke of heaven, but He also warned of hell (Luke 16:19-31; Matt. 25:46).

Odds and Ends

Joe believed that one of the wonders of the world was the seedless watermelon! He also—

• Recognized the importance of computers but wanted nothing to do with them. When asked what his Internet address was, he would reply, *www.don'tcare.com.*

• Loved fireplaces and campfires. Said if he hadn't become a preacher, he might have been an arsonist!

• Collected all kinds of walking canes. He made a few himself.

• Wore size 9 1/2 cowboy boots for dress wear.

• Was 5 feet 7 1/2 inches tall.

• Hat size—7 3/4.

• Very left-handed. Quipped, "I would give my right arm to be ambidextrous."

• Possessed a Concealed Handgun License.

• Through the years raised a number of dairy calves for the freezer. Raised a couple of cows after he retired. Raised coturnix quail a time or two.

• Periodically battled kidney stones. Drank distilled water

and tea made from it. Seemed to help him in his later years. One of his favorite verses: Luke 6:1, "And it came to pass."

• He didn't eat them all the time, but a couple of his old-time favorites were licorice candy and gingersnap cookies.

• After retirement, besides preaching, he maintained a lawn-mowing business for a couple of years.

• Believed in the Baptist Faith & Message 2000, the doctrinal statement of the Southern Baptist Convention.

• Enjoyed knives and sharpening knives. He could put a razor edge on one so that it would shave the hair on your arm.

• As a boy, had the nicknames Columbus and Cotton. Cotton was because of the white hair he had as a boy.

• As a boy, thought the Oshman's Sporting Goods Store in Bay City was about the finest store in the world.

• Loved the mountains. Loved the sound of seagulls.

Lose Them to the Cause or Lose the Cause to Them

In the early 1960s a doctrinal controversy arose in the SBC over a Bible commentary written by a liberal professor at Midwestern Baptist Theological Seminary, Kansas City. (The school since has changed. Now all professors believe in the inerrancy of the Bible.) Some worried that if we take too strong a stand on the inerrancy of the Bible, we might lose some of the more liberal scholars to our convention. I remember Dad telling me of a response he appreciated from K. Owen White, pastor of First Baptist Church, Houston, and Convention president in 1963-64. As I remember Dad telling it, White said, "We would rather lose them to the cause than to lose the cause to them."

Menudo or Jesus?

Through the years Joe invited evangelist Larry Taylor to preach for several revivals. Larry had grown up in San Antonio, TX, and had become a pool hustler and drug addict before he got saved. Larry also admitted to having a taste for menudo (a Mexican food dish.) No one is sure what all is put in menudo!

But stories abound of blood and guts and who knows what.

On one occasion Joe looked the evangelist in the eyes and without cracking a smile said, "Larry, don't you think it's about time you gave up your menudo for Jesus?" Later, when they would run into each other at conferences, Larry would laugh and say, "Joe, I've finally given up menudo for Jesus."

On a much more serious note, Larry told me about a time he and Joe went into a barbershop and about how Joe witnessed to the barber. As Joe told the barber about Jesus, sin, heaven and hell, he noticed a water faucet that was slowly dripping. Joe reached over and got a drop of water on his finger. He told the story that Jesus Christ told in Luke 16 of the rich man and Lazarus—how the rich man found himself in hell tormented in flames. The rich man begged for Abraham to dip his finger in water to cool his tongue. Larry said that Joe held his finger up with the drop of water dangling from his fingertip as he told that barber of the horrors of hell but also of the love and forgiveness that Jesus has to offer when we come to Him. Larry said he will always remember how Joe witnessed to that barber that day so long ago.

Seeking After a Sign

In traveling, Joe relied heavily on Bonnie to give him directions. She never missed a road sign; he often did.

When she would try to get him to pay more attention to the traffic signs, he would reply in his dry, sarcastic way, "An evil generation seeks after a sign" (Matt. 12:39).

Say That Again?

Joe thoroughly enjoyed the story told to him by C. S. Mincy, a relative from Mississippi. As C. S. and his wife traveled in Arkansas, they looked for a store. Back in the hills they finally located one. C. S. told his wife, "Wait in the car. I'll go in and see if it's clean and likely to have what we need." He went in and saw that it was fine. He told the man behind the counter,

"My wife is about to come in and do some shopping. She is just about deaf; she can't hear thunder. You have to just about scream at her for her to hear." Actually her hearing was fine.

Then he went to the car. "The store's OK," he told his wife, "but the man behind the counter is just about deaf. You have to scream at him to make him hear."

He later said his wife and the merchant screaming at each other was one of the funniest things he ever saw.

Airplanes over Damon
When Joe was a boy, especially in the Damon area, airplanes were uncommon. Joe recalls that in the rare event that an airplane flew over the schoolhouse, the teacher would permit all the kids to go to the window to watch it fly by.

Healing Powers of the Seventh Son
Eldridge Perry (Bud) Brumbelow's twin brother was Ailbert. No one was sure which of the two was the seventh son of their father, Martin Van Buren Brumbelow. But an old wives tale said that a seventh son could rub a wart and the wart would go away. Folks approached Bud and Ailbert for their medical help. Bud didn't put much stock in the tale, but he had a lot of fun trying to help folks out. He supposed it did about as much good on warts as did any other remedies.

I also heard an old, true story of Bud and Ailbert: one of them took a girl to a party, and the other one took her home. She never knew the difference.

Grandpa—Indians, Bear Hunting, Catfishing
Joe's dad, E. P. Brumbelow, was born in 1881 and lived to 1975. He saw the last days of the Old West and grew up in a different world. As a boy he saw a band of Indians, some on horseback and some walking down the road toward them in central Texas. They stopped; one asked Bud's dad, Martin Van Buren Brumbelow, if he had any tobacco. He produced a plug. The

127

Indians passed it around, each taking a chaw (bite). They then went on their way. Bud said that they were the only "wild" Indians he had ever seen.

Black Bears are just now returning to the western portion of Texas from Mexico. They had been killed out of Texas in the early 1900s. Bud hunted some of those last bears. He told of once arriving at the camp of Theodore Roosevelt. He did not get to see him. Roosevelt and those accompanying him had been there so recently, however, that Bud said their campfire still had warm embers. Bud hunted bears in the Brazoria County area. He showed Joe where he had killed a bear close to Old Ocean. He told of killing a bear at Sugar Valley in Matagorda County.

Eldridge Perry Brumbelow and his twin brother, Ailbert, went hunting. One of them killed a bear as it ran and raised up to attack the other. They later found that she had two cubs. Each brother took one to raise. They enjoyed the cubs until they began to grow up and become mean. They would break into the house and get the milk or syrup and make a mess. Ailbert gave his bear to a zoo in Houston or Richmond.

One day after E. P. had milked the cow, his bear came up and slapped the bucket out of his hand. He whipped the bear; it climbed up a tree and stayed for a couple of days. It finally got so mean that E.P. gave it to Mr. George, who had an enclosed area for some wild animals.

I wish I remembered more details of the following story Joe told of his Dad: Joe told of how Bud and his twin brother, Ailbert, found themselves on Big Creek without any fishing gear. They wanted to put out a throw line for catfish. They found a little bit of string but could not find a hook. Dad told how they got a straight pin, bent it, tied it on the end of the line. They caught a grasshopper for bait. They returned later to find a huge catfish on the line. The fish wasn't moving or pulling. They carefully got hold of it and then examined the hook and line. Apparently the catfish had swallowed the bait and hook; the hook got tangled in its gut. Ordinarily the catfish easily could have pulled off such a line, but the hook (pin) was in such a sensitive place the catfish would not pull.

About 1899 Grandpa and a brother rode their horses down to the Damon area from Blooming Grove, TX, a distance of about 250 miles. They liked what they saw, so they rode back and told their folks. Their parents liked what they heard, so they moved from the Blooming Grove-Frost, TX, area down to Brazoria County.

Bears and Fur Trade in Early Texas

This was before Grandpa's time when far more black bears were in Texas. The early fur trade in Texas might be of interest to some. "Around 1830, no less than 40,000 deer hides, 1,500 bearskins, 1,200 otter pelts, and 600 beaver pelts passed into the hands of Nacogdoches (TX) merchants in only a few months" (*Backwoodsmen* by Thad Sitton, University of Oklahoma Press: Norman and London; 1995, p. 168.)

Martin Van Buren Brumbelow

Bud's dad, Martin Van Buren Brumbelow, was born in 1840 and died in 1925. He moved from Gibson County, TN, to Navarro County, TX.

He served in the Civil War beginning in 1861. He served his time in Texas as a gunner. Joe's sister, Myrtle, adds, "Dad's father was stationed at the old fort near Velasco, TX. They patrolled the beach but never killed a Yankee. Once when they camped on the beach, a Yankee gunboat was sitting just out of gunshot range. The Confederates killed a cow and were cooking it over a campfire. The Yankees yelled out about how good it smelled. They said they were really hungry but declined an invitation to surrender and eat.

"The commander told them the war was over and to go home. M. V. B. Brumbelow walked back to Blooming Grove, TX." From Velasco to Blooming Grove was a distance of about 250 miles.

Martin returned from the Civil War ready to marry his childhood sweetheart, Sarah Jane Green. His future father-in-law was not ready. Martin wrote the following poem to tell the story:

"It was evening, it was moonlight
It was late and it was fair
I was courting, I was happy
I was brave for she was there.

She was pretty, she was blushing
She was willing to be wed.
He arrived and he objected
He was Papa so I fled.

I returned, he was repentant
She was coaxing her Mama.
He relented and I thanked him
And forgave him dear Papa.

Then he blessed us
I was happy, while she was blushing a rosy red
He was willing, she was willing
I was willing, we were wed."

Martin and Sarah were married November 8, 1865. The rest is history. Martin's poem was taken from an article written on Martin and Sarah Brumbelow's 50th wedding anniversary by Charles L. Rawson of Fresno, TX. Rawson's grandfather was a brother to Martin Van Buren Brumbelow.

Scared By a Bear
An old tale says that if a woman is terribly frightened by something when she is pregnant, her child will take on some characteristic of what frightened her. Joe testified that this was true. When his mother was carrying him, she was frightened by a bear. Sure enough, he was born with bare feet.

Toilets—Outdoor and Indoor

Joe and his family grew up during the days of outdoor toilets. His Dad, Bud, was born in 1881 and did not know anything about an indoor toilet until late in life. He opposed them. He said, "It's just not right to do that in someone's house. I'm not going outdoors indoors." He was living with his son, Bill, who was building a new house. Against Bud's protests, Bill included an indoor toilet. Bud, however, was won over. He finally concluded that an indoor toilet was one of the finest things around.

Preaching Along the Same Lines

Hershel Ford was a great Baptist pastor who published many sermon books. Without naming names, some preachers were known to "borrow" Ford's sermons. Ford was aware of this and welcomed it. He said, "If my books can be of help to you, you are welcome to the sermons." Joe had a preacher friend who bought Ford's books and "borrowed" the sermons on a regular basis.

This pastor had a church member who moved to El Paso, TX, and joined Hershel Ford's First Baptist Church. The man later moved back and rejoined his old church. Joe's preacher friend asked the returning member, "What was it like at First Baptist Church, El Paso?" "It was great," the member said. "How did you like Hershel Ford's preaching?" The man replied "Brother Ford is a great preacher. As a matter of fact, he preaches a lot along the same lines as you do." The preacher never confessed.

Streaker in the Old Folks' Home

Things were getting dull in the Old Folks' Home. Finally, to liven things up, a resident took off her clothes and ran through the middle of the reception area. "Was that Mildred?" one resident asked another. "I think it was." "What was she wearing?" "I don't know for certain, but it sure needed to be ironed."

The German Spy

When Joe was a boy growing up in Damon during World War II, everyone naturally was concerned about the war. Joe remembered his parents listening to the radio news. With a look of concern, they sometimes shook their heads and said they didn't know how things were going to turn out.

The best thing about a small town is that everybody knows everybody. The worst thing about a small town is that everybody knows everybody. Rumor was that an old German man in town was a German spy and that he had a two-way radio hidden in his attic. He reported directly to Adolf Hitler on a regular basis, people said.

Looking back, Joe laughed about the rumors, saying, "Even if he had been a spy, why would Hitler care about what was going on in Damon, Texas?"

What a Pastor Needs

Delphia and Dick Jackson, my aunt and uncle, heard Pastor John Hatch tell this in one of the church services years ago. I know Dad enjoyed it.

A pastor needs three things: gray hair to make him look mature, eyeglasses to make him look scholarly, and a case of hemorrhoids to make him look concerned.

Advantage I Never Had

Sometimes friends gave Joe a tough time by telling him that one of his sons preached better than he did. Joe would reply, "That may be true, but there's a reason for it. They have had a great advantage that I never had. As they grew up they sat under my preaching for 18 years."

Barbers and Marriage

Preachers walk a tight rope when the subject of marriage and divorce are concerned. On the one hand, they are to preach in favor of marriage and against divorce. They should tell how God hates divorce, of all the negative consequences that result, and how that God wants a strong, happy marriage. On the other hand, if someone has been divorced, a preacher needs to convey God's forgiveness and acceptance, whatever their past. Finding the proper balance is difficult. Sometimes, no matter how conscientious and plain the preacher is in his premarital and marital counseling, he still gets the blame.

When Joe returned to Houston to be a pastor, he visited a local barber shop. As he cut Joe's hair, the barber realized he knew Joe from years ago. He began to tell all his customers that this preacher was the one who married him. He would conclude by laughingly saying, "He must not have tied a very good knot. We got divorced." Each time Joe would get his hair cut, he went through the same ordeal.

Finally Joe had enough. For what seemed like the hundredth time the barber was telling everyone that the preacher had not tied a very good knot. Joe replied, "I'll tell you one thing. When you got married, there were some solemn vows made to God and everyone present. Somebody lied, and it wasn't the preacher."

The barber never brought up the subject again.

Comments on Joe Brumbelow by His Older Sister, Myrtle Mae (Brumbelow) Montier

"Joe began his public school education in 1935 at age 5. His father was 49 years old when Joe was born and wanted to be sure he saw him finish high school. He paid a monthly fee to the school so his under-age son could enter the first grade. Miss Newcomb (or Newcome) told the students the story of Columbus; then at a later time she asked them to retell it. Joe's version was the best. He was taken to each elementary classroom to tell the story. I was so proud when he came to our 5th-grade class. Many older kids called him Columbus.

"We walked about a mile to school, often with others. We had raincoats and boots when needed. Lunches mostly were biscuits with sausage, ham, and peanut butter and jelly or apple butter.

"Joe's mother was buried on the first day of his second year in school. Sometime later that school year his great-grandfather, John J. Hudgins, died. Joe and Bill Brumbelow (Joe's brother) were born on June 20th as was John J. Hudgins in 1851. Most years we celebrated their birthdays and Father's Day at Oyster Creek, Texas, where John J. lived. Our grandmother, Addie Follett, and her family—her sister, Amelia, and brother, Buster— were there. It was a big family event. Children played under the house in the dirt and got very dirty. The house was above the ground two or three feet.

"Joe was born in Rosenberg, TX, in an upstairs apartment belonging to the Ralstons.

"During the 1932 storm we were in a house belonging to Aunt Cordelia and Uncle Leon's son. Our house was lifted up off the blocks and gently set down. A brick chimney didn't break and a burning kerosene lamp didn't fall. It felt like we were floating. Joe, of course, didn't remember, as he was sleeping on a pallet in the living room where our parents were.

"We lived across the hill (where Bill was born) from present-day Damon when Daddy's sister, Mary, and her husband, Ben Price, came to stay with us sometime in the 1930s because he had a broken leg. A pulley was placed near the ceiling with a rope so he could elevate his leg to relieve the pain. Joe was about 4 or 5 years old then and a good talker. Uncle Ben said he would be a good preacher. Uncle Ben's papers (Preacher's Journal, religious literature) were left for Joe. Of course, Joe did become a preacher.

"After our mother died, Aunt Cordelia (Dad's sister) and Uncle Leon Langston stayed with us and Daddy worked away from home three nights a week. Joe would argue. He often was in trouble with them because his arguing was considered talking back or sassing. His father had to paddle him for his misbehaving—mostly talking back, I think.

"The Langstons were older than Daddy, so they were unable to work too long taking care of us kids. Several other people tried to help with the kids but didn't last long.

"Wadie Bingham, who lived with her daughter, Emma Lea Allen, became the housekeeper. They were our closest neighbors; she had been a friend of our mother's. Her grandchildren, near our age, called her Mom, as we eventually did. She and Dad were married about three years after our mother died.

"Daddy's job was walking the pipeline from Damon to Pasadena to check for oil leaks. This took him several days. He would spend a night with Uncle Ailbert (Brumbelow), a night with a black man and his wife on the Brazos River, and a night somewhere else. He returned to Damon on a late-afternoon train. He often walked home from the train stop in Damon (since we then lived across the hill, it was about a mile or so to walk), but sometimes we went to meet him in the car.

"He also walked the pipeline from Damon to Boling. We took the car to Boling to meet him. Daddy had purchased a 1939 two-door Chevrolet from Roy Wright Chevrolet in West Columbia. It cost $765.

"He worked for Sinclair several years. Once the company wouldn't cut the brush in the right-of-way above the pipeline. Daddy quit after being struck at his boot top by a rattle snake. That was sometime in Joe's young childhood and the Depression years. Daddy sold our car and bought a dump truck. He did some hauling and finally got a job with the county. He went to Angleton to pick up relief supplies and take them to distribution places. He brought some to Damon also.

"We were not on relief, but many were. We were not ever hungry. We always had a cow or two, hogs, a garden, and wild game and fish.

"As a young boy, Joe loved hunting and fishing and dogs.

"Still in Damon, we moved to the house next to the post office in 1939. Daddy owned the house and land. Before, we had rented wherever we lived, except in 1933 Daddy bought the house across the hill but paid $12 a year for rent of the land.

"Raymond and Bruce Goode seemed to be Joe's best friends after we moved next to the post office. Bill and Joe and the

Goode boys roamed around Damon. They skinny-dipped in a pond somewhere, but their parents never knew.

"Toys for the boys were a wagon, tricycles, marbles, tops, balls and bats, and B.B. guns. Joe was probably a teen-ager before he had a bike. He cut grass to earn money for it.

"Since we lived next to the telephone office (we lived between the post office and the telephone office), Joe sometimes earned money by going to someone's home to tell that person he or she had a call. They had to go to the telephone office and call back. Sometimes the woman at the telephone office paid him 10 or 25 cents. If he had to walk a mile or more, the pay was $1.

"I was gone from home before he was in high school. His behavior, such as the skunk odor on his boots, etc., caused problems for his teachers. (See chapter 10, "Skunks, Boots, and The Schoolhouse Furnace.")

"Sunday School and church were always a part of life in Damon. Some years we went to church in nearby West Columbia. We never had a regular, live-in Damon preacher; they usually came only on Sunday."

—Myrtle Mae (Brumbelow) Montier, Port Lavaca, TX, 2004

Chapter 9

"Good God, They Shot Grandma!"

Joe was asked to officiate at a funeral in Corpus Christi; the burial was to be in Alice. As Joe and the funeral director rode to Alice together, they exchanged some stories. The funeral director told Joe the following story as the absolute truth:

The funeral director conducted a funeral for a veteran. At the conclusion of the graveside service they gave a 21-gun salute. When the guns sounded, an older woman at the front was so overwhelmed with grief, she fainted and fell to the ground. A little boy in his coat and tie cried out, "Good God, they shot Grandma!"

Bob Thrift and TV

Early in Joe's ministry television was a new thing. People were buying TV's like crazy.

In the early days some preachers did not believe in having a television and preached against them. Bob Thrift was one of those preachers and sometimes chided Joe in a friendly way for not preaching against television. Joe did not own one, mainly because he could not afford it. But he said that while he did not own one (at that time), he just had never felt led to preach against them.

Sometime later, just before the Texas Evangelism Conference in Fort Worth, Joe got word that Bob had bought a TV. After an evening conference session a group of preachers stood in the hallway. They had been moved by the great preaching and singing. Bob Thrift said to the group, "Why don't we go to one of our rooms and have a prayer meeting?" He turned and said,

"Can you be there, Joe?" Joe replied, "No, Bob, I can't. You see, I have a hotel room with a big TV. I don't have one at home, so I've got to take advantage of it while I can."

Bob laughed and admitted he had purchased a TV. "I knew you were going to get me; I just didn't know when."

Six Abreast

Joe's dad, Bud, did not care much for the big city of Houston. On one of his infrequent trips to Houston, Dad was driving Grandpa on one of the Houston freeways. Remember, this was a man who was born long before automobiles existed. He was from a small, country town. As they entered the freeway, Grandpa tensed up, grabbed what he could, and exclaimed, "Watch out Joe, they're coming six abreast!"

Grandpa also used to muse, "This many folks don't have any business being on the road."

When Grandpa was up in years, he still cared about going hunting and fishing, or at least looking things over. He and Dad would check out places like Big Creek and the Brazos and San Bernard rivers. They would drive over some old, wooden bridges and close to some steep, washed-out banks along the rivers. Grandpa would get scared every time they approached such places. Dad would try to get as close to the edge as he possibly could, just to agitate Grandpa more.

In Dad's later years, we boys did the same thing to him. He would tense up and say, "You're getting too close." Of course, it always looks worse to the passenger. When he would get onto us, we would remind him that it was payback for the way he used to treat his own dad!

Charbon and Dipping Vats

Much has been heard in recent days about terrorism and anthrax. Most do not know that anthrax has been around for many, many years. Joe said the name for it when he was growing up was charbon and it could wipe out the cattle business in any area it struck. Apparently charbon can stay alive in the ground for many years. I looked it up in an older dictionary and found charbon as another name for anthrax.

Texas is cattle country. Joe remembered mostly commercial and "bremmer" (Brahman) cows back then in the Damon area. He told about the dipping vats they prepared for cattle. People filled the vats with water and mixed in medicine, insecticide, or who knows what. Then they would run the cattle through the vat. Joe said they would take their dog down to the working pens and throw him in the vat. He said it would cure the dog of mange, fleas, or whatever might be ailing him.

Those Folks Have Got It Made

Joe picked cotton just enough to know it was not his calling. He mentioned that as a kid picking cotton he occasionally would see a car driving down the highway with cane poles sticking out of the window. The people in the car clearly were going fishing for the day. To that boy back then, that was a perfect picture of someone who had it made!

Thank You Lord, But . . .

Much rain had fallen on the north side of Houston. This was in the 1950s. Doverside Baptist Church did not have adequate parking. Folks were having to walk through the mud and ankle-deep water to get inside. The rain fell . . . and fell . . . and fell.

The ushers went to the front of the church to receive the Sunday-morning offering. Joe called on one to lead the offertory prayer. As humbly and sincerely as he could be, the usher prayed, "Lord, we thank You for the rain. We just didn't know we needed so much."

Burr Oaks and Shotgun Shells

When they were kids, Joe and Bill planted a burr oak tree behind their house in Damon. Burr Oaks have big acorns and are tough, long-lived trees. Today it's a big, beautiful tree. The

139

Yelderman Cemetery (1616 Stockwell, Damon, TX. GPS: 29 degrees 17.318 N; 095 degrees 44.833 W) did not allow trees to be planted in the cemetery, but we got permission to plant one just outside the fence close to Joe's grave. We thought planting one there would be appropriate.

One day I went to check on the tree and found a shotgun shell lying on his gravestone. We never knew where it came from. Mom mentioned that everyone in the area knew how he and the Brumbelows loved to hunt. Growing up, Joe had hunted all over that area. Bonnie decided it could have been most anyone in that part of the country. Nothing could have been more appropriate to put on his grave!

Right or Wrong?

This is a study Joe used with youth and adults:

The Bible is the Word of God—completely true. The Bible is our guide. If the Bible says it's wrong, it's wrong.

But what about the things (such as smoking, drugs, etc.) to which the Bible does not directly speak? Several biblical principles guide us:

1. Will it offend someone else? (Rom. 14:21; 1 Cor. 8:9) Will it be a stumbling block to someone? Lead that person astray? Hurt your Christian influence?

2. Is it doubtful? (Rom. 14:23) We usually don't have doubts about things that obviously are right and moral.

A man looked at a shirt he previously had worn, held it up, smelled it, then said to his wife, "Honey, is this shirt OK to wear again?" She replied, "Remember, if it's doubtful, it's dirty."

3. Can you honestly thank God for it? (1 Thess. 5:18)

4. Is it harmful to your body? (1 Cor. 6:19-20)

5. Will it glorify God? (1 Cor. 10:31)

6. Will it help or hurt your walk with God? Will it bring you closer to God, or pull you further away from Him?

7. Would you like to be doing it when Jesus returns? (Matt. 24:44)

When the Lord Leads

Joe once called a preacher to ask him to preach a revival for him at Dawson. The preacher had gotten more spiritual than the last time Joe had used him. He explained to Joe that he did not take revival dates as they arrived, as most preachers do. Instead, he said he laid the invitations out before the Lord and asked the Lord which ones he should accept. Since he couldn't get a straight answer about whether the preacher would preach or not, Joe just dropped the matter.

A year or two later, after Joe had moved to Corpus Christi to be pastor of West Heights Baptist Church, a letter was forwarded to him from Dawson. It was from this preacher. The Lord now had given him permission to preach a revival for Joe at Dawson.

The preacher had assured Joe that he only went at the Lord's leading. Joe was sure that the Lord knew he had moved to Corpus Christi; therefore, Joe assumed the preacher must have gotten his wires crossed up somewhere. Sometimes we can just get a little too spiritual.

Insert Where Needed

Joe was not the best at the finer points of grammar, punctuation, etc. Bonnie never went to college, but she had made excellent grades in high school and knew the basics of grammar. When Joe completed a college research paper, he would give it to Bonnie to type. At the bottom of his research paper he was known to have written a row or two of periods, commas, quotation marks, colons, and semicolons. He then wrote, "Please insert these where needed."

How's Virginia Doing?

Joe went to college with Tom Clawson. They were lifelong friends. Those who just casually knew them thought they looked similar and sometimes got them mixed up. I'm sure Joe would have claimed that he was much better looking than was Tom! Tom's wife was Virginia; Joe's wife was Bonnie. Through the years at conventions, occasionally someone would mistakenly ask Tom, "How's Bonnie doing?" Sometimes Joe would be asked, "How's Virginia doing?" They joked about how they finally just started saying, "Oh, she's doing fine."

A Loving God Wouldn't Send Anyone to Hell

Occasionally someone would say to Joe, "A loving God would not send anyone to hell." Joe sometimes would respond with this illustration:

Suppose your medical doctor told you that you were dying and had no hope. You replied, "Is there no hope? Doctor, you can't just let me die." Suppose you begged and pleaded with the doctor until he said, "I know of just one hope—a very rare and expensive medicine, but I know you never could afford it." You replied, "Doctor, please let me live. You've got to get me that medicine."

Suppose the doctor took pity on you and determined he was going to obtain that medicine, no matter the cost. The doctor sold his house, sold his car, and anything else he had of value. Then he borrowed all the money he could, even though it would put him in debt for the rest of his life. Finally he scraped the money together and gave it all to buy you that vial of costly medicine.

The doctor arrives with the medicine and tells you how much it cost him. "My wife and children will be in poverty from now on, but we couldn't let you die," he tells you. He then carefully hands you the precious vial of medicine.

Suppose you looked at that vial of medicine in disdain and then threw it to the floor. The doctor watches in horror as the vial that cost him everything breaks; the medicine runs into the floor.

Then suppose you had the audacity to say, "Doctor, you're not just going to let me die, are you? I thought you loved me more than that."

You were a sinner headed for hell. But God loved you and gave His only begotten Son—the most precious thing He had. Jesus went to the cross for you. He shed His royal blood, gave

142

His life for you, and then rose again. Because of the incredible sacrifice Jesus made for you on Calvary, you simply can accept Him as Lord and Savior and be forgiven and escape hell. But you reject the most precious gift that has ever been given and then have the audacity to say, "How could a loving God send someone like me to hell?"

It Was the Governor

Years ago when Ohio Governor Nash was in office, a terrible crime was committed in the state of Ohio. A beautiful young woman was found murdered. She was from a prominent family and had been dating a young man from a prominent family. All evidence pointed to the man—Jim. Jim was accused, tried, and found guilty. He was sentenced to die by hanging and was placed in a maximum security prison.

Many people tried to talk with Governor Nash about commuting the sentence, a pardon, or any means of sparing Jim's life. Nash was a business-like man. He always dressed in a black suit and tie with a white shirt. Some said he looked just like a preacher. He would give the same answer to those who tried to persuade him to change his mind: "Jim had a fair trial. A jury has convicted and sentenced him."

As a last effort, Jim's mother, who actually knew Governor Nash, visited him. She was admitted to his office. When she entered, all she could do was fall on her knees and weep. The governor was very moved. He placed his hand on her shoulder and said, "I'll talk to Jim."

Nash went to the prison. Admitted to death row, he approached Jim's cell and said, "Jim, I want to talk with you." Jim looked up and saw what he thought was another preacher. Jim responded, "Go away; I don't want to talk with anyone." But Jim, I think I can help you." "Go away," replied Jim. "Nobody can help me." "But please, just let me talk with you." Jim again replied, "Nobody can help me. Now go away and leave me alone." With that, the governor turned and left.

After he had left, the warden approached Jim's cell and asked, "Well Jim, how did you make out with the governor?" "The governor? I haven't seen the governor." The warden said, "Jim, that man that I let in to see you was Governor Nash."

Jim began pacing back and forth in his cell saying, "My God, it was the governor; he wanted to help me, and I wouldn't let him." Over and over he repeated the same words, day after day, week after week. "My God, it was the governor; he wanted to help me, and I wouldn't let him." The day arrived for Jim to be led to the gallows. When asked if he had some last words, he spoke in a hoarse whisper. Only those closest to him could make out the words, "My God, it was the governor; he wanted to help me, and I wouldn't let him."

Those who refuse Jesus and His gift of eternal life one day will say, "It was Jesus; He wanted to save me, and I wouldn't let Him."

The Other Side of the Cemetery

A pastor drove out into the countryside to visit the Hendrix family. He knew the general area, but did not know exactly where they lived. This was back in the days when roads were not always paved and travel could be difficult. The pastor noticed the road becoming smaller and smaller. The pavement appeared to end soon.

He saw a young boy on the side of the road, stopped, and asked if he knew the Hendrix family. The boy knew them well and was glad to give directions.

"Mister," the boy said, "You just stay right on this road. It will lead you to a cemetery. The road goes right through the middle of the cemetery. After you get through the cemetery, they will be down the road a way—the third house on the right."

The pastor thanked him. As he was about to leave, the boy added, "Mister, the road gets mighty bad between here and the cemetery. There are some potholes. The road may get muddy and rough. You might even get stuck. But when you get through the cemetery, you've got it made. It's a paved road after that."

For the Christian, the road can get narrow and difficult. Bumps and potholes are there to navigate. And the road leads right through the middle of the cemetery. But when we get through the cemetery, we've got it made.

The Bible teaches, "To be absent from the body and to be present with the Lord" (2 Cor. 5:8). "Having a desire to depart and be with Christ, which is far better" (Phil. 1:23). "For to me, to live is Christ, and to die is gain" (Phil. 1:21).

Sam Houston Teaches a Preacher a Thing or Two

Sam Houston is famous in Texas. On April 21, 1836, he defeated General Santa Anna at San Jacinto, thereby winning independence for Texas. The San Jacinto Battleground is just about five miles and across the Lynchburg Ferry from where I live in Highlands. It is just a few miles east of the city that bears Sam's name. He became president, and later governor, of Texas. Before moving to Texas, Houston fought in the War of 1812, served in the United States Congress, was governor of Tennessee, and lived for a while with the Cherokee Indians. Sam was not exactly a Christian man during his early days. The Indians gave him a nickname, "The Big Drunk." Later in life his wife was instrumental in leading him to the Lord. Sam Houston was baptized by Rufus C. Burleson in Little Rocky Creek at Independence, TX, in 1854. Burleson had previously arrived from Alabama as a Southern Baptist missionary to Texas. He was a preacher, Baptist leader, and president of Baylor University. Burleson and Houston became close friends.

About five years later, Independence Baptist Church was entangled in a huge controversy. Unfortunately, Christians can and occasionally do act in an ungodly manner. The church and community were embroiled in controversy. A crucial church vote did not go the way Brother Burleson thought it should. Burleson pitched a fit. To the moderator and pastor, Brother Ross, Burleson said publicly some very unkind words. Ross then dismissed the service.

That evening General Houston was sitting with a friend when Burleson walked in and extended his hand to Houston. Houston stood and crossed his arms behind him. Then Houston began to tell of serving amid controversies in Tennessee, the United States legislature, the Cherokee Council, and tumultuous days in Texas. Houston said, "But during all my public life I have never seen such improprieties in the proceeding of any body, as you were guilty of this morning in the Baptist church, when you shook your finger in Brother Ross' face, charged him with dishonorable conduct, and told him that nothing but his gray hairs protected him from personal violence. You baptized me in Rocky Creek in 1854, and in your company I have spent many happy hours in social and spiritual enjoyment. For many years I have been your devoted friend. But, Brother Burleson, after witnessing your conduct this morning, you must excuse me, but I cannot, I will not, take your hand until convinced that you have sincerely repented." Burleson bowed himself out of the office and went home.

Things seemed to calm down. A few weeks later Independence Baptist Church had a Protracted Meeting (what revival meetings once were called). The evangelist, Rev. Stribbling, preached for nearly a week, but the services seemed dead. Stribbling then said, "Brethren, this meeting is not progressing as I, and I trust you all, prayed. We are not right before God, or He would send us a blessing. Let us all get down on our knees and join with Brother Burleson in an earnest prayer that God will remove all obstacles in the way and send us down from heaven such a blessing as our souls are not able to contain."

Almost all present quietly fell to their knees. Burleson was wearing his finest dress clothes. Under tremendous conviction he rose and humbly asked their forgiveness for his behavior.

He then said, "Brother Stribbling, you have asked me to kneel in prayer. This I cannot do. I feel like prostrating myself in the dust of this earth and ask Him to take everything away that hinders, or in any way interferes, with the progress of this meeting."

146

With that, this eminent preacher and educator walked to the aisle and fell forward to the floor, with his face in his hands. As he lay on the floor, he began to pray. In the language of that day, this was said of his prayer of confession: "This prayer was the most soulful ever heard. The stone walls were almost melted. It reached the very Throne, and moved the Almighty God Himself. The windows and doors of Heaven were thrown wide open, and copious showers of Divine blessings descended upon that town, that had been torn and tossed on the waves of internal strife for years."

After the service, Dr. Ross and others gave Dr. Burleson their hand of Christian fellowship and reconciliation. Sam Houston said, "Brother Burleson, here is my hand. Hold it while life lasts. Here is my heart; it will love you with its last pulsation."

That is what true revival is all about.

—Illustration used by Joe Brumbelow. Most of the information from *The Life And Writings of Rufus C. Burleson*, compiled and published by Mrs. Georgia J. Burleson; 1901.

I Know That's in the Bible

Surprisingly we assume many things are in the Bible, when they just aren't there. This is even true of those who know the Bible quite well. Joe heard well-known preachers preach about the Death Angel at the first Passover. Joe preached on the Death Angel until he realized the Bible does not mention him in Exodus. God said, "When I see the blood, I will pass over you."

Like many others, Joe preached about Jesus' falling beneath the weight of the cross. But as he studied, he found that the Bible never mentions Jesus' falling on the way to Calvary. You may assume He did because of Jesus' physical condition and because Simon of Cyrene was compelled to carry Jesus' cross. The Bible, however, does not say anything about Jesus' falling.

The same is true about the Christmas story. Joe and Bonnie prepared a test that emphasized the importance of knowing what the Bible really says, rather than reading our assumptions into the Bible. The test was, "How Well Do You Know The Christmas Story?" The test follows; answers follow the test.

1. Where was Jesus born?
2. How did Mary and Joseph get to the place of Jesus' birth?
3. What animals were at the manger scene?
4. Were the wise men at the manger scene?
5. How many wise men (magi) were there?
6. In what year was Jesus born?
7. On what month and day was Jesus born?
8. Who sang at Jesus birth?
9. What does the name Jesus mean?
10. Who tried to kill the baby Jesus?
11. Where is the Christmas story found in the Bible?

Answers: 1. Bethlehem, just outside of Jerusalem. 2. The Bible does not say, despite most people's believing that Mary rode a donkey led by Joseph. We assume that because of pictures and movies. 3. The Bible doesn't name any. We can assume they were there because it was a barn or stable. And, of course, there had to be the donkey that Mary rode! 4. Probably not. The Bible says they came to the house where Joseph, Mary, and Jesus were. It may have been as much as a year or two after the birth of Jesus. 5. The Bible does not say. It refers to them in the plural, more than one is assumed. I suppose we assume three because three gifts were received. The Bible also does not give the names of the wise men. 6. Our current calendar, made in the middle ages, intended the year as AD 1. The calendar, however, was off several years. We still do not know for sure what year Jesus was born, but it could not have been after 4 BC. We know from history that Herod the Great, who tried to kill Jesus, died in that year. Jesus was probably born about 5 BC, before Christ! AD does not mean after dead; it is the abbreviation of a Latin term that means, "In The Year of Our Lord." 7. We don't know for sure; the Bible doesn't say. 8. No one. The Bible refers to the angels *saying* "Glory to God in the highest." 9. Savior, Deliverer. 10. Herod,

148

known in history as Herod the Great. 11. Mainly in Matthew 1-2, and Luke 1-2.

The solution to knowing whether something is really in the Bible or not? Read it for yourself!

Floundering at Midnight

Years ago Baptists, and Christians in general, were much more particular about observing Sunday as a day of rest and worship. Blue Laws required businesses to close on Saturday or Sunday, so their employees could have a day of rest and/or worship. Since all businesses (except hospitals, etc.) had to be closed, no unfair competition existed. Good Christian folk did not take well to one of their own desecrating the Sabbath. Certainly fishing or hunting or being involved in sports on Sunday was frowned on.

In the early 1960s when Joe was pastor in Corpus Christi, it was close to good fishing on Padre Island and Packery Channel. You did not have the strict fishing laws we have today. Joe literally would fill up a long stringer with speckled trout and a few redfish and flounder thrown in. He did this while wade-fishing. One of his secrets was that he was fast about reeling the fish in, putting it on the stringer, rebaiting with a live shrimp, and casting out again. The more time you have a hook in the water, the more fish you're going to catch. He did not even want to take time to wade back to shore and get another stringer, so he would get us boys to wade out to him and give him an empty stringer and maybe something to drink. Then we would get his full stringer and bring it back to shore. The fish never were wasted. Family and friends consumed them.

Joe also went floundering. This involves fishing at night with a lantern, a gig, and a stringer. Flounder are flat fish with both eyes on one side of their head. They are some of the best-tasting fish to eat. At night flounder will move up into the shallow salt water and bed down into the sand. You wade in water about a foot or two deep and look at the bottom with the aid of the

149

lantern. Your gig, usually two-pronged, is at the ready. When you see the outline of the flounder, you stick the gig in him, then hold him down until you can carefully grab him and put him on the stringer. After you have been through a certain area, you can wait two or three hours to let other flounder have time to move in and cover the same territory again.

Dad did not fish on Sunday. I remember, however, times back then when, after church Sunday night, he would gather his floundering equipment. We would drive to Padre Island and, since it was Sunday night, we would wait until midnight. A couple of minutes after midnight, Dad would start floundering for the night.

In Bible times, a day was measured from sundown to sundown. The new day would begin at sundown rather than at midnight, so why couldn't he go fishing at sundown on Sunday? Somehow, I don't think Dad could have convinced those old-time Baptists of that detail.

(The Jewish Sabbath was the seventh day, or Saturday [Deuteronomy 5:12-15].) Many years ago, however, Christians referred to Sunday as the Sabbath or the Christian Sabbath. It is also referred to as the first day of the week and the Lord's Day Matt. 28:1-6; 1 Cor. 16:2; Rev. 1:10).

A Nickel in the Hand

A boy was playing with his friend and thought of a dare: "I have a nickel. If you can get it out of my hand, you can have it." His friend tried and tried, to no avail. Finally, the friend managed to pry open one finger. Then he was about to get another finger open. The little boy with the nickel jumped up, ran into the house, and got his father's help. The father's big, strong hand was placed over the boy's hand, with the nickel still inside. No matter how hard the friend tried, he could not get the father's hand open. The nickel was secure.

Joe used this story to explain the concept of eternal security: Jesus gives eternal life to His sheep. He said they will never perish. Jesus then said that no one can take them out of His hand. But even if someone could, Jesus said, "My Father is greater than all, and no one is able to snatch them out of My Father's hand" (John 10:27-29).The believer is safe in the arms of Jesus.

Other Scripture Brother Joe used to present the eternal security of the believer: John 3:16; 5:24; Ephesians 1:12-14; 4:30; 1 Peter 1:5; Jude 24; Psalm 37:24; Romans 8:35-39; 2 Timothy 1:12; John 14:16; 1 John 5:13.

Chapter 10

Change

People were hosting a birthday party for a 90-year-old man. Someone at the party said to him, "I suppose you've seen a lot of changes in your lifetime." The old man replied, "Yep, and I've been agin' every one of them."

Three Letters

A pastor arrived at a church known for trouble and for short pastorates. The previous pastor contacted the new pastor. He said, "I've prepared three letters for you and left them in the pastor's office. They are sealed and don't need to be opened yet." The former pastor continued, "Things will go great for you for two or three months. Then the honeymoon will end, people will start complaining, and everything will seem to go wrong. When that happens, open envelope number one. The next crisis, envelope number two. The third crisis, envelope number three."

Sure enough, things went great for the new pastor for three months or so. Then the church started complaining. Everything was going wrong. The pastor remembered the three letters and opened the first. It said, "Blame me." The next Sunday the pastor said, "You know, things are in a mess around here. But I'll tell you why. It's because of that no-good, former pastor. He really fouled things up." The people said, "You know, he's right. That no-count pastor really made a mess of things." That seemed to calm things down. The church went along smoothly for a while; then another crisis occurred.

The pastor opened letter number two. It said, "Blame the deacons." The first letter had worked so well, he decided to try it. Next Sunday the pastor said, "We have problems here again. People are divided and complaining. But the reason is because of the deacons around here. They're just not doing their job. They've got things in a real mess." The church folks said, "That's right. The deacons aren't worth much in this church." Things went great for a few more months; then it happened again—another big church fight. The pastor went back to his office. He opened letter number three. It said, "Prepare three letters."

Worthy Is the Lamb

Three major Christian views exist about the Second Coming of Jesus Christ. The three views are amillennial, postmillennial, and premillennial—the last being the correct view! Joe was a premillennialist, though he had good friends who did not agree with him on all these details.

All three views agree that Jesus will return, a resurrection and final judgement will occur, and we will have an eternity either in heaven or in hell. Amillennialists believe that no literal millennial reign of Christ will occur on the earth and that all of the above basically happens at once. Postmillennialists believe that a millennium of peace and advance of the gospel occurs first, then Jesus returns. Premillennialists believe that the rapture happens first, then seven years of tribulation on earth, the battle of Armageddon, then Christ returns to reign for 1,000 years (the Millennium) of peace on earth. Many variations of the premillennial view exist, but the one just stated is the basic one that Joe believed.

Premillennialists believe that the biblical prophecy concerning the Second Coming will be fulfilled literally, just as the prophecy concerning the First Coming (birth of Jesus in Bethlehem, earthly life, and ministry of Jesus) was fulfilled literally. Premillennialists do agree that the Bible contains symbolism, but they interpret Bible prophecy more literally than do those of some other viewpoints.

While Southern Baptists will argue over the details, we will then all go out to eat together. But, of course, Baptists do like to argue and give each other a friendly jibe now and then.

I think it was R. G. Lee who Joe heard say years ago that he was so premillennial that he would not even say "Ah" when he went to see the doctor. Lee joked that he was so premillennial he would not eat "Post" Toasties® for breakfast.

In college Joe had to read and review the book, *Worthy Is the Lamb,* by Ray Summers. This book takes a strong amillennial view of the book of Revelation. Joe's professor also was amillennial. I don't know if he wrote this in his paper, but later Joe would say, "About the only thing I agreed with in the book was that the Lamb is worthy!"

(Read more about it. Good premillennial authors include: H. A. Ironside, Warren Weirsbe, Adrian Rogers, John Walvoord, W. A. Criswell, J. Vernon McGee, C. I. Scofield. In Scripture Jesus is referred to as the Lamb of God in Rev. 5; John 1:29.)

Uncle Ben Price

Joe's preacher uncle, B. N. (Ben) Price, was married to E. P. (Bud) Brumbelow's sister, Mary. He performed the wedding ceremony of E. P. and Carrie Mae (Follett) in 1925. He died when Joe was a boy. Ben left some of his personal items for Joe, even though Joe was just a lad. Ben told his parents that Joe was going to be a preacher, so he wanted to give those things for them to keep until Joe was older. Joe never knew that Uncle Ben believed he would be a preacher. Joe's sister, Myrtle, told us after Joe's death.

That may be the best way for a family to deal with the issue of one of its boys being a preacher. Don't pressure him. If God wants him to be a preacher of the gospel, God will let him know.

B. N. Price was born in 1860 and was saved in 1879. In his journal he records being baptized by Elder Leek and joining the church at Spring Dale, Jack County, TX. He was ordained to preach May 10, 1891.

B. N. Price worked in the Baptist Missionary Association and also among Southern Baptists. In July, 1902 Ben Price recorded his previous eight months' labor in the Missionary Association. His report included: Days Labor 193; Sermons 107; Miles Traveled 2,023; Homes Visited 663; Sunday Schools Organized 9; Bibles Sold 151; Bibles Given Away 19; Books Sold 251; Books Given Away 25; Prayer Meetings Conducted 6; Public Prayers 86; Private Prayers 51; Public Appeals 56; Personal Appeals 53; Tracts Given Away 1,482; Conversions 38; Churches Organized 3; Baptized 12; Public Collections 40; Money Collected $170.55; Received by Letter 8.

Among one of his orders in 1902 were the books: *Pilgrims Progress* 17 cts.; *Black Beauty* 20 cts.; *Theodosia*, vol. 1; *Little Baptist* 40 cts.; *In His Steps* 20 cts.; New Testament, Psalms 35 cts.; also complete Bibles with indexes.

In 1900 a note appears in his journal with no further comment. It says, "Storm blew away", a reference to the Galveston hurricane that brought such devastation and took more than 6,000 lives. Joe Brumbelow's grandmother—his mother's mother—lived through and wrote about this hurricane. After the hurricane Joe's dad, E. P., helped bury bodies of those who had died in the hurricane or who had been washed out of their graves by the storm surge.

Included in Ben Price's possessions was a brochure of a Bible conference at the Texas Baptist Encampment at Palacios—the encampment at which Joe Brumbelow later would surrender to the ministry. The camp brochure was from about 1920. One comment in the brochure assured the reader that a paved road was all the way from Houston to Palacios. That was a big selling point back then.

A Canoe, A Barge, and the Intercoastal Canal

In the mid 1990s Joe, his son, Mark, and Mark's wife, Cherry, decided to go floundering. They drove to the mouth of the San Bernard River. From there they just had to go about 100

155

or 200 yards across the Intercoastal Canal to the island. They did this before dark, spent the night floundering and camping around a campfire, then returned the next morning. They did not have a boat available. Since they had only a short way to go, they borrowed my 16-foot aluminum Osagian canoe. They got across without incident.

The Intercoastal Canal is a coastal waterway protected from the rough waters of the Gulf of Mexico by a series of long, narrow islands. It is well-used by sportsmen as well as by industry. They have tugboats pushing one or more large barges loaded with all types of cargo.

The next morning before daylight Joe, Mark, and Cherry loaded the canoe; all three got in; and they began to paddle their way back across the Intercoastal Canal. They noticed a barge approaching in the distance, but it was far away; they had plenty of time. As they approached the middle of the canal, they took note that they were going slower. The barge was approaching faster than they had realized. The barge was so big and high compared to the canoe. It probably could have run right over them, and the tugboat captain never would have known that anything happened. Like a train, the barge could not have stopped in time even if it had known about the canoe. They began to paddle faster. The barge got bigger and bigger. Then they could feel the suction as the huge barge began to displace the water around it and them. Things seemed to happen in slow motion as they paddled for their lives. They seemed to be making no progress at all in the face of the behemoth that bore down on them.

They survived to flounder another day. I was not present, but that is one scene I would have loved to behold. Next time you're on the Intercoastal Canal, watch out for those barges. Even if you're right and they're wrong; they're bigger.

Bulls and Quail

Aldon Nesmith was a faithful deacon at First Baptist Church of Dawson. He was the first man that Lester Roloff, in his early

156

ministry, had led to the Lord. Aldon was a farmer and rancher and was "laid back" in everything he did.

Joe had not done any quail hunting to speak of before he moved to Dawson in 1976, other than maybe walking up on quail accidentally while he hunted something else. Quail hunting was big in Dawson. The joke was that you might mess around with a man's other property and get away with it, but you had better not bring harm to his birddog. For those not up on quail hunting, it is usually done with a dog. The dog finds and points them, then the hunter eases up with his shotgun, flushes them, and shoots. Quail usually huddle in a covey in the brush or weeds on the ground until someone walks right up on them. Then they will suddenly, noisily fly up. Even when you know what's going to happen, they can still scare you. Joe went quail hunting with Dawson folks like Mike McReynolds, Don Mitchum, and probably several others.

The first time Joe went quail hunting, it was with Mike McReynolds. Snow fell that first day of quail season. Joe had grown up on the Gulf Coast where snow was rare. He was excited because this was his first time to go quail hunting and his first time to hunt in the snow.

One day Joe decided to go quail hunting on his own on Aldon Nesmith's property. He could tell Aldon really wanted to join him, but Aldon had work to do. He had just loaded a big bull onto a small cattle trailer. The single bull was so big, it filled up the little trailer. Aldon said he'd had so much trouble penning and loading the bull that he had to go ahead and take the bull to the auction. With longing in his eyes he went back to the truck and trailer while Joe began his hunting.

As Joe hunted, he saw Aldon in the distance as he began the drive through the pasture. The bull was not happy about being penned. It was snorting and pitching a fit in the trailer. When the truck was about halfway to the gate and road, Joe saw the bull make a mighty leap. It jumped right out of the top and over the side of the trailer and went on its way in the pasture.

Aldon was calm and collected. He went back to his house, got his shotgun, and joined his pastor in his pursuit of quail.

Sam Houston's Conversion and Its Results

Sam Houston—general, president, senator, and governor of Texas—was a great man politically, but also had been a great sinner. During a presidential race a Texas newspaper referred to Houston as a wreck, but a noble wreck. His wife, Margaret, had been a consistent Christian witness to him. Many could not believe it when, after a long struggle, he trusted Jesus Christ as his Savior. Houston was baptized November 19, 1854, in the chilly waters of Rocky Creek near Independence, TX. You have to be serious to be baptized outdoors toward the end of November!

"The announcement of General Houston's immersion," recounted a church periodical of wide repute, "has excited the wonder and surprise of many who have supposed that he was 'past praying for' but it is no marvel to us . . . Three thousand and fifty clergymen have been praying for him ever since the Nebraska outrage in the Senate."—quote from *The Raven* by Marquis James, 1929.

A friend said to Houston, "Well, General, I hear your sins were washed away." Sam Houston replied, "I hope so. But if they were all washed away, the Lord help the fish down below."

After his baptism by Independence Baptist Church, Sam Houston engaged to pay half of Pastor Rufus C. Burleson's salary. Houston explained, "My pocketbook was baptized, too."

General Houston and John H. Reagan were traveling on horseback shortly after Houston's baptism. Houston's horse stumbled and Sam cursed. Reagan, his traveling companion, appeared shocked. Realizing what he had done, Houston got off his horse, knelt in the road, and asked God for forgiveness. (Information from various sources including R. C. Burleson, Joe Tom Davis, Marquis James.)

158

Small Treble Hooks

Joe used live shrimp and small treble hooks to fish in saltwater. A man once wandered up where Joe was fishing. He saw the small treble hooks and announced to anyone who would listen that you can't catch anything with that small a hook.

A couple of minutes later Joe pulled in a prize speckled trout. Holding it up for the expert to see, he declared, "That's what you can catch with those little hooks."

Ed Young for President

The year that Ed Young, pastor of Second Baptist Church, Houston, was elected president of the Southern Baptist Convention, my brother, Stephen, and I attended the SBC. Everyone knew that Young was to be nominated for the presidency. The day before Young was elected president, during Pastors Conference, we ran into Ed Young in the hallway. We said hello and Ed Young asked, "Where's your dad?" Steve replied, "He stayed home. He just couldn't get excited about anyone running for president this year." Ed laughed and said, "I don't blame him."

Dad would want me to add, just for the record, that if he had attended that year, he would have voted for Ed Young.

Designer Jewels

When we boys got older, Mom worked outside the home. One of her jobs was with Designer Jewels in Houston. A Jewish man, Bobby Sandler, and his son, Mark, owned the business. Dad would sometimes drive Mom to work. Both of them got to know and love the Sandlers. Bobby occasionally went to Europe on business. While there he would buy samples of chocolate to determine which ones were best to use as gifts for some of his customers. This was before Joe's diabetes. Joe kindly offered to sample the chocolate to help out Bobby.

Joe humorously got onto Bobby about the contemporary art decorating the walls of Designer Jewels. He told Bobby he could hang the paintings upside down and no one would know the difference.

Years later we were honored to have Bobby and Adele Sandler attend Dad's memorial service. If you ever need a good deal on jewelry, give Bobby or Mark a call. They are listed in Appendix 1. If you need good art, look elsewhere.

Phat Physicians
Joe figured out how to find a good medical doctor. Find a fat doctor; he won't bother you too much about your own weight.

I should add, however, that Dr. J. E. B. Johnson was not fat; he became one of Joe's favorite doctors.

Skunks, Boots, and the Schoolhouse Furnace
Growing up in Damon, Joe, Raymond Goode, and some others for whom I do not have names trapped some skunks. After much delicate work they collected a small bottle of skunk scent, which later was poured on the furnace at the Damon School. The aroma filled the schoolhouse. Reports still are fuzzy as to exactly which boy carried out the deed.

During the process of dealing with the skunks, Joe got some of the scent on his black boots. They smelled to high heaven. He claimed that he tried his best to get the smell off. They were his good boots that he had to wear to school. In those days you did not just throw away an otherwise good pair of footwear. They certainly did not have the money to go buy another pair.

Joe finally got the smell off the boots. Later he discovered that if the boots warmed up near the school furnace, the smell would return. Occasionally he would make a point to sit or stand near the furnace and really stink up the place. Bob Glasgow said the teacher would make Joe go sit out in the hall and added, "This is probably what he wanted to do." Some of the old Damon students still talk about the smell of his boots at school.

Right Foot, Left Foot

Joe told of Mr. Peg Pingleton in Damon, who had a missing right leg. I don't have confirmation, but the story was that Pingleton got to know another man who was missing a left leg. Once or twice a year they would go to town to buy, and share, a new pair of shoes.

Attempted Murder of a School Teacher

The doors of the classrooms in the Damon School were divided in the middle with a two-by-four (piece of lumber) that would drop down from the upper section to lock them together. The schoolteacher, Mrs. Martin (Ward), was after Joe Brumbelow and Raymond Goode for some misdeed. Raymond ran out the door, dropping the two-by-four as he went. Mrs. Ward ran into the two-by-four. Joe could see the humor in lots of things. He could not help laughing at the sight. The teacher was convinced this was premeditated and that Raymond intended the two-by-four to fall and hit her squarely on the head.

As the teacher related the story, "Raymond tried to kill me and Joe laughed about it." I think Raymond and Joe did suffer rather severe consequences for that encounter. They were allowed to stay in school, though. The teacher left and declared she never would come back to the school to teach as long as Joe Brumbelow and Raymond Goode were there.

Many years later, Joe would preach Raymond Goode's funeral. Raymond was buried at the Damon Cemetery. After the service, Raymond's younger brother, Bruce, approached Joe and said, "I want the straight of the story. Was it like Raymond always told me—that the schoolteacher accused Raymond of trying to kill her and you laughed about it?" Joe admitted to Bruce that was the straight of the story.

Lying or a Bad Memory

After Joe retired, he was preaching in a church in Brazoria County when an older woman approached him after the service, introduced herself as Mrs. Martin, and said, "I used to be your schoolteacher at Damon." Yes, she was the schoolteacher mentioned above. Joe remembered her well; they had a pleasant conversation. She then stayed at the front of the church and announced to the members as they exited, "I used to teach Brother Joe in school. He was one of my best students."

The part about being one of her best students—Joe said he appreciated the comment, but the schoolteacher either must have been lying or had a bad memory.

Running Those Hogs Off the Cliff

The Damon Baptist Church used to be a half-time church. One Sunday a Baptist preacher would preach; the next Sunday a Methodist preacher would preach. Later it became a full-time church in the sense that it called a Baptist preacher who could be there every Sunday. The church still could not pay a pastor a full-time salary; the pastors they had usually lived in Houston and drove down to Damon on Sundays.

Some preachers, if they're not careful, can be guilty of preaching the same thing week after week. We are to preach the entire Word of God, not just our favorite verses. One of the Damon pastors was guilty of this. One of his favorite Bible stories was that of Jesus casting the demons out of the maniac of Gadera. The demons were cast into a herd of swine. The hogs, then in a crazed state, ran off a cliff into the Sea of Galilee (Mark 5:1-20).

Joe's dad was sick one Sunday and could not attend church. After the rest of the family returned from church (yes, the rest of the family can actually attend church when one member of the family is sick!), Bud asked what the preacher preached on that morning. Joe's little brother, Bill, (who was exactly three years younger than Joe; they had the same birthday), spoke up, "Oh, he just ran those hogs off the cliff again."

Accumulation of Wealth Does Not Bring Happiness
In 1923, a group of the world's most successful financiers met in the Edgewater Beach Hotel in Chicago. Present were:
President of world's largest independent steel company
President of the largest utility company
President of New York Stock Exchange
The greatest wheat speculator
The greatest Bear in Wall Street
A member of the President's Cabinet
Head of world's greatest monopoly
Collectively they controlled more wealth than was in the U.S. Treasury.

25 Years Later

President of world's largest steel company, Charles Schwab, lived on borrowed money last five years of his life and died penniless.

Greatest wheat speculator, Arthur Cutten, died abroad insolvent.

President of New York Stock Exchange, Richard Whitney, was released from Sing Sing Prison.

Greatest Bear in Wall Street, Jesse Livermore, committed suicide.

Member of President's Cabinet, Albert Fall, was released from prison so he could die at home.

Head of world s greatest monopoly, Ivor Krueger, committed suicide.

President of Bank of International Settlement, Leon Frazier, committed suicide.

Wealth brings sorrows—Christ brings peace.

A man can endure poverty better than prosperity.

(—from an old tract; later copied on flyleaf of Joe's Bible)

Most Preachers Are Honest, But . . .
The Bible teaches we are to be sober and discerning. It even speaks about the gift of discernment. Shortly after Joe moved to

Doverside Baptist Church in 1955, a man showed up one Sunday morning. He was familiar with many of the members and at one time had been a member at Doverside.

The people were impressed with his exploits and asked Brother Joe if he could be allowed to get up during the service and share about his ministry. The man got up and told about what seemed to be an outstanding Christian ministry. He even told of how he had been working with the Billy Graham Evangelistic Association and had filled the pulpit for Billy. This was after the Billy Graham revivals had begun to sweep our country.

Naturally, some were very impressed. One woman, who happened to be a schoolteacher, was carried away and thought he was just wonderful. Some, however, were a little suspicious. Joe and one or two of the deacons decided to check out his story. They found out that this preacher's story was entirely fabricated. He was not in any type of ministry.

Sometimes checking the references pays.

The Youth Evangelist

After Dad retired, he stayed busy preaching and was called to speak to a senior citizens church group. He mused, "I used to be asked to preach youth revivals." I replied, "But you're still preaching to the same crowd." He laughed and agreed.

A Church Can Get Ripped Off

When Joe was pastor of Bethel Baptist Church in Corpus Christi, TX, in the mid-1960s, a husband and wife attended one Sunday morning for the first time. At the invitation they both came forward to receive Christ as Savior. They seemed sincere. They returned that Sunday night—usually a sign of real commitment.

The man asked one of the deacons he had met that morning if he could talk with the deacons and pastor after church. At that meeting he told them he had been trying to think of all the things

164

he had to get right in his life, now that he was a Christian. He was the accountant for a car dealer in town and confessed that he had been embezzling money. He had talked to his boss that afternoon. The boss told him that he would lose his job, but if he paid back the money immediately, he would not press charges. Through tears he told of how no one would loan him the money under those circumstances.

A sympathetic deacon suggested that all the deacons and pastor co-sign a loan for him. The deacon knew a banker that would agree to such a loan. The deacons were all in favor; Joe hesitantly went along.

After the meeting, the man gave Joe a nice pen and pencil set in a fancy box. He said that was all he had to show his appreciation and he would assure them that the loan would not cost one of them a penny. Joe later said, "That was the most expensive pen and pencil set I ever received, because the man disappeared without paying one cent on that loan." Joe and Bonnie had to struggle to pay off their part of the loan. That was one of the difficult lessons learned by a minister and deacons.

Pastor, if you're caught in such a situation, make sure it's just the deacons who co-sign the loan!

Football and Homeruns

While at Dawson, TX, Joe preached one Sunday morning about getting excited about serving the Lord. On the way home from church, he mentioned to Bonnie that he was surprised how Hershel Montgomery had acted in church. A faithful member, Hershel typically didn't laugh through the church service.

Bonnie answered, "I'll tell you why. In your sermon you were telling how excited people get over sports. You said, 'You go to a football game and cheer and holler when someone hits a homerun.'"

In that Sunday-evening service Joe explained that he knew the difference between a touchdown and a homerun. He did confess that he never had been accused of being a great athlete. He said, "The closest I ever came to being an athlete was twice having athlete's foot."

And the Name Is . . .

As most pastors do, Joe preached many funerals during his ministry. He preached the funerals of several people who had been murdered in what folks used to call the bloody northside of Houston. Funerals were an emotional drain for Brother Joe, but he was glad to try to be a comfort to the family and loved ones. It also gave him a chance to preach to some who did not normally attend church. His funeral sermons were brief, but he always presented comfort from God's Word and how the people left behind could be sure they were going to heaven.

Years ago in Houston, Joe was faced with an unusual situation. A man who, as a young person, had been in his church started running with the wrong crowd. He was convicted of a crime and sent to prison for several years. When released, he found getting a job with his record to be difficult, so he legally changed his name. He married and had a child. His wife knew him by his new name, though she also knew his history.

He died as a fairly young adult. His brothers and sister did not even know his name had been changed. The older brother emphatically stated that he would not sit through the funeral service if his new name were used. The wife emphatically stated that she would not sit in the service if the old name were used.

After prayer and direction from the Lord, for the first and only time, Joe preached a person's funeral service without ever using the person's name. Throughout the service Brother Joe referred to him as "your loved one", "our friend", etc. Everyone seemed satisfied with the service.

A Motorcycle Gang Funeral

A wonderful Christian older couple were members of Joe's church in Houston. They had a wayward son whom Joe had never met. He was a member of a notorious motorcycle gang. He was involved in a bad accident while not wearing a helmet. The young man was in the hospital for days before his death.

His parents said, "Brother Joe, we know you didn't know our son, but we'd like you to preach his funeral." Joe was glad to help the couple. He then learned of the funeral plans.

The motorcycle gang wanted to pay for all funeral expenses. They also wanted to provide the music, pallbearers, etc. They did agree, however, for the parents' pastor to speak.

The members of the gang all had nicknames. The fellow who died had the nickname of "Crazy."

As people arrived for the funeral, Patsy Cline's song *Crazy* was playing loudly. After a while, they changed the tape to the song: "He was born the next of kin, the next of kin to the way-ward wind." About 100 motorcycles were at the service. When they went to the graveside, the gang rode their cycles right up on the grass all around the grave. They also were carrying their cartons of beer, their radios, and who knows what else. They had all kinds of notes and mementos to put into the casket or to throw into the grave.

After Joe led in a brief graveside Scripture reading and prayer, the funeral director insisted that the parents and other family members leave. The gang had plans to lower the casket and close the grave. To those hesitant to leave before the closure, the director explained to them some of the unique, final practices of the motorcycle gang. After hearing of those practices that will not be detailed here, they were glad to leave.

A Hook in the Ear

In the early 1960s Joe Brumbelow was preaching a revival in Corpus Christi and went fishing with Francis Williams and Pastor Joe Kayser. In the course of their fishing trip, Francis cast his rod and reel while too close to Kayser. The hook on his line impaled Kayser's ear. The barb on the hook makes such an incident more complicated, so they decided the prudent thing to do would be to go to the doctor. Williams was a sensitive, caring sort of fellow and felt terrible about hooking his pastor's ear. All three ended up in the doctor's office. Kayser was hurting; Williams was apologizing and fretting; Brumbelow was trying not to see the humor in the situation.

The doctor began working on Kayser's ear as Kayser lay on the table. Every time the doctor would get hold of it, Kayser would cry out in pain. His legs would involuntarily lift off the table. Williams was feeling more guilty all the time. Brumbelow was trying to look concerned.

Picture, if you will, the following repetitious scene: The doctor would get hold of the ear. Kayser would groan and his legs would rise from the table. Williams would fret, express regret, and wring his hands all the more.

Brumbelow couldn't take it any more. In spite of his concern and the obvious pain, he had to leave the doctor's office. He couldn't contain his laughter any longer.

(Francis Williams was a layman in Bethel Baptist Church, Corpus Christi. He later would serve as pastor in Louisiana. In recent years he confessed that while his heart went out to Kayser at the time, he also was trying not to laugh.)

Chapter 11

Of Geese and Storms

Joe would point out to an unsuspecting soul how geese would always fly in a "V" formation. Then he would ask, "Have you noticed that one side of the 'V' is always longer than the other side?" "Yes," they would say. "Do you know why?" Thinking they were about to receive some little-known information on wildlife behavior, they would expectantly say, "No, I don't. Why?" Joe replied, "Because there's more geese on one side than on the other side."

Joe would relate how bad a recent storm was: It blew down trees that never had blown down before.

Too Poor Not to Tithe

On occasion someone would make the comment, "I'm too poor to tithe." Joe would respond, "I'm too poor not to tithe. God promises to bless those who tithe both materially and spiritually. I'm too poor to get by without the blessings of God that we receive from tithing." Joe also said, "Sometimes people say they are on a fixed income and cannot tithe. The compassionate thing would seem to be to tell them they don't need to worry about giving to the church and to the Lord. But God promises to bless and provide for those who give tithes and offerings. I discovered that I would be holding back the blessings of God on their lives if I told them they did not need to tithe."

Denying Me a Blessing

At times when Brother Joe Brumbelow felt led to give to a particular person in need, but the person would refuse to take the gift, Joe would say, "God led me to give you this. He promises to bless those who give. Are you going to deny me a blessing from God by refusing to accept my gift?" Few refused a gift from Joe after that explanation.

(Sermon Notes) How I Know the Bible Is God's Word
2 Timothy 3:16; 2 Peter 1:21; Matthew 5:18

I. Miraculous Preservation

"Hammer and Anvil"

Robert Ingersoll, famous infidel of the 1800s, said in 15 years this Book (Bible) will be in the morgue.

Voltaire said in 100 years this Book would be outmoded and forgotten; would be found only in museums.

Instead, after Voltaire's death, his house was purchased and used as a warehouse to distribute Bibles.

II. Miraculous Agreement

66 books in Bible, written by some 40 men, over a period of 1,500 years. Human authors from all walks of life—from kings to peasants. In all the Bible, there is agreement and no contradictions.

Today you could get 40 men from the same church, same background, same financial and social standing to write on their impressions of God. It would have many contradictions.

III. Universal Acceptance

Bible is a best-seller in Japan, China, Germany; all over the world it speaks to the hearts of men and women.

IV. Prophetic Accuracy (Prophecy about the birth and life of Jesus Christ)

1. Virgin Birth of Christ—prophesied 700 years before birth of Jesus in Bethlehem. Isaiah 7:14. (B.C.=Before Christ)

2. Born in Bethlehem. Micah 5:2 (about 710 BC)

3. Slaughter of Children. Jeremiah 31:15 (606 BC)

4. Flight into Egypt. Hosea 11:1 (740 BC)

5. Miracles—eyes opened, ears opened, lame lifted. Isaiah 35:5-6 (700 BC)

170

6. Betrayed by a friend. Psalm 41:9 (About 1000 BC)

7. Price paid for Jesus (30 pieces of silver). Zechariah 11:12 (487 BC)

8. Use of money. Zechariah 11:13 (487 BC)

9. Crucifixion. Psalm 22:16 (circa 1000 BC)

10. Gambling. Psalm 22:18 (c. 1000 BC)

11. No bones broken. Psalm 34:20 (c. 1000 BC)

12. Died with wicked, buried with rich. Isaiah 53:9 (712 BC)

V. Scientific Accuracy

Bible not a book of science? Yes, it is. The more science learns, the more it falls in line with Bible teachings. Bible not strictly a book of science, but when it speaks to scientific matters, and properly understood, it speaks the truth.

1. For many years medical doctors bled patients. They thought they had too much blood. Red swirl in barber's pole originally stood for "bloodletting performed here." George Washington was bled. Then scientists made remarkable discovery—blood is the life of the body.

God said that 3,500 years ago (Lev. 17:11).

2. World round

Galileo proclaimed as heretic.

Columbus determined to reach India by sailing westward. Called a crackpot and fool.

They made an amazing discovery—the world is round. Isaiah 40:22

3. World out in space supported by nothing.

Ancients believed world supported by elephant or turtle. God said, Job 26:7.

4. Modern science discovered human body made of same 16 elements as found in ordinary soil of earth (Gen. 2:7; 3:19).

VI. The Words of this Book Satisfy

The evolutionist, agnostic, or philosopher cannot give the answer to life and the origin of world. This Book does. First words, "In the beginning God created the heavens and the earth."

VII. What I've Seen The Bible Do

Uncle Charlie, Utsey, Weaver. (Personal testimonies of people whose lives had been changed by God's Word.)

Bible says you are a sinner, you are going to perish in hell. Bible also says God loves you; Jesus died for you; you can be saved, forgiven. This Book can change your life!

(Notes from sermon Joe Brumbelow preached Feb. 5, 1968, at First Baptist Church, Cypress, TX. Some folks said this was one of his best sermons.)

There is a time, I know not when,
A place, I know not where,
Which marks the destiny of men
To Heaven or despair.

There is a line by us not seen
Which crosses every path,
The hidden boundary between
God's patience and His wrath.

To cross that limit is to die,
To die, as if by stealth,
It may not pale the beaming eye,
Nor quench the glowing health.

The conscience may be still at ease,
The spirit light and gay,
That which is pleasing still may please
And care be thrust away.

But on that forehead God hath set
Indelibly a mark,
By man unseen, for man as yet
Is blind and in the dark.

And still the doomed man's path below
    May bloom as Eden bloomed,
He did not, does not, will not know,
    Nor feel that he is doomed.

He feels, he sees that all is well,
    His every fear is calmed,
He lives, he dies, he wakes in Hell,
    Not only doomed, but damned.

Oh, where is that mysterious bourn
    By which each path is crossed,
Beyond which God Himself hath sworn
    That he who goes is lost?

How long may man go on in sin,
    How long will God forbear?
Where does hope end, and where begin
    The confines of despair?

One answer from those skies is sent,
    "Ye who from God depart,
While it is called today, repent,
    And harden not your heart."

—Dr. J. Addison Alexander

from *The Best Loved Poems of the American People*, selected by Hazel Felleman
(New York: Doubleday, 1936).

Arctic Circle

When Joe was in Alaska, he became close friends with
Pastor Jim Clark. Jim recently said he always had great revivals
with Joe in Alaska and later in Jackson Hole, WY, and that he
grew to love him like a brother. While in Alaska Jim had to fly to
Chalkitsik, above the Arctic Circle, to check on a mission there.
Jim was a pilot (Alaska has more pilots per capita than does any

173

other state), but another man was piloting this plane. Joe flew with them and enjoyed seeing some wildlife on the way.

Jim asked the pilot if his plane bumped, like his did, when it crossed the Arctic Circle. The pilot said it did. As they passed it, sure enough, they felt a definite bump.

Joe called Bonnie back in Texas to tell her about his trip. He was fascinated with the Arctic Circle and the airplane bump. One of his sons expressed some skepticism about the bump. Bonnie asked him what caused it. Joe turned to Jim Clark and asked him what caused the bump as they flew across the Arctic Circle. Jim replied, "The pilot." Jim said he watched as Joe's face turned red.

Mother's Day

Joe's mama, Carrie Mae, died when he was about 6; he did not have many clear memories of her. Later his dad married Wadie. Joe grew to love his stepmother. She served for several years as church clerk at Damon Baptist Church. He called her Mom; she died when he was a teen-ager. Joe's dad went to heaven in 1975. On Mother's Day, May 14, 1978, at First Baptist Church, Dawson, TX, Joe read a letter he wrote to his mom.

Dear Mom,

It's Mother's Day. Some of my church members are gone to see their mothers. Others have made long distance calls and written letters. It's been nearly 30 years since you moved to heaven. I know that you can see real clearly from there and don't need a letter. But just the same I thought I'd like to write and thank you better than I ever did while you were here for what you did and what you were.

I'm glad you believed in discipline. I remember the time I laughed and talked with Raymond during church and disturbed the service. You sure knew how to handle that. I never did it again.

I remember how you used to read the Bible to me and then we would get on our knees and pray. Sometimes my knees got

174

tired, but you built a wall around my soul that the devil never has been able to tear down.

I remember the time I overheard you crying in your room and praying for me when I had really fouled up—you didn't know I heard you, but it meant so much to me to know that somebody cared.

I was just thinking about when I was away from home and surrendered my life to preach the gospel of Christ. I thought how surprised you'd be when I told you. When I broke the news to you, you weren't surprised at all, but you wept and said you had been expecting it for a long time. You made me promise to be faithful and never quit. When I look back over the road and see how close I've come to quitting sometimes, I know that your prayers must have followed me. Mom, do you remember how you used to sing all the time while you were cooking or ironing and you were so concerned because I couldn't learn to carry a tune? Well, I never did learn, but when I move over there, I'll have a brand new voice and we'll sing together that song you loved so much, "Amazing Grace."

How's Dad liking heaven? I sure have missed him since he moved over there. I know he enjoys being able to walk again and think clearly again. For months here he talked of going on home to heaven. Tell him hello for me and that I think of him nearly every day.

Thanks again for being firm and loving and Christian. From the looks of things down here, it won't be long till Jesus comes. I'll see you in the morning.

Love,
Joe

Uncle Charlie

As a college student Joe was pastor of the Baptist church at Clegg, a community in South Texas between George West and Freer. He drove there from Corpus Christi each Sunday. It was a small church filled with some wonderful saints of God. Joe learned of a couple of older men who lived in the area who were known as some of the meanest, most anti-Christian folks around. One of them, Uncle Charlie Latham, had said, "I'd just as soon shoot a preacher as a rattlesnake."

Joe said, "I'm going to visit them next Sunday." A member of the church said, "If you do, let us know first. We want to know where to look for you if you disappear." Next Sunday Joe went to see them and found they were not at home. Uncle Charlie had had a stroke and was in the hospital at Beeville. Joe went to the hospital and was surprised that Charlie seemed glad to see him. Joe told him about the plan of salvation and led him to accept Jesus as his Savior. The people of Clegg could hardly believe it. A man who had been one of the meanest men around had experienced a radical change in his life. Charlie was moved from the hospital to a nursing home. A nurse who had not known Charlie before later told Joe that Uncle Charlie was "such a nice man."

That's one of the reasons Joe knew that the Bible and Jesus Christ can change lives.

Fiddler's Island

As a boy Joe and his family sometimes traveled to the mouth of the San Bernard River, where it empties into the Gulf of Mexico. They would fish, flounder, camp out, and maybe gather oysters. Close to the mouth of the San Bernard is Fiddler's Island. At night a faint, peculiar violin sound at times is heard in the area. The story was that a man who played the fiddle drowned there or that his true love died or left him. In despair he cast himself into the waters.

Grandpa (E. P. Brumbelow) explained that the sound is probably made when the tide waters run through the shallow beds of oysters. Or, could it be the playing of the fiddler's ghost?

Outdoor Stories

People eat strange things. The strangeness often depends on our own culture and background. While eating possum has never

176

caught on, a few country folks do eat them. Joe turned up his nose at the thought of someone eating a possum. He explained why: "Once when I was hunting. I found the carcass of a cow. I walked up and kicked it. Three possums ran out from the inside of that carcass. Every time I think of eating a possum, I think of those possums eating inside that rotten cow."

Joe told that when he was a kid, a poor family moved into an abandoned house way back in the woods. They were there a year or so and then moved on. Joe hunted in that area after the family had moved away and found armadillo shells scattered all over the front yard. Apparently the family had practically lived on armadillos the whole time they were there.

As Joe went hunting with his dad, his dad used the opportunity to lecture him on snakes and how dangerous they are—to watch where he stepped and look out for them. Their area had four poisonous snakes: rattlesnakes, copperheads, coral snakes, and cottonmouths or water moccasins.

After the lecture and some hunting, they sat down on a rotting log to rest. As they stood up, Joe looked down and saw a small rattlesnake that his dad had sat on. It had been pressed down into the soft, rotting wood. Joe didn't let his Dad forget about his unobservant behavior.

Joe once shot a squirrel; when he went to get it, he found two dead squirrels. A second had been hidden in the grass but in the line of fire of his shotgun.

Joe told about his family's hog hunting with a pack of dogs. A hog got hold of the dogs and really ripped them up. They had their bellies slashed; one or two had their intestines exposed. Joe said his dad took a regular needle and thread and sewed the dogs' bellies up. The dogs completely recovered.

When he was a teen-ager, Joe was hunting way back in the woods and had no water to drink. He finally decided to drink out of a creek whose waters looked reasonably clear. After drinking his fill, he walked a little further upstream and found a rotting, maggot-infested, carcass of a cow lying in the edge of the creek.

If you ever drink out of a creek, never walk upstream.

When Joe was pastor of Bethel Baptist Church, Corpus Christi, he went wade-fishing in the surf. The fishing wasn't much good; he only caught three whiting and put them on a fish stringer he kept tied to his belt. Only when he waded to shore did he notice he now had two-and-a-half whiting. A shark had bitten off half of one of his fish.

Joe could skin a squirrel making only one cut. He made the cut under the tail and through the tailbone, then standing on the base of the tail, holding the rear legs and pulling up.

Once he set a perch trap under water. The wire cage had funnels that guide the fish in to get the bait; then they can't find the opening to swim out. We went to check the trap and were startled to find a big water snake in the trap. The snake was dead. It apparently had seen the fish, swam in to eat them, then could not find its way out.

Ham and Ramsey

Mordecai Ham was one of the great evangelists of the turn of the last century. Joe's dad, E. P. (Bud) Brumbelow, had some memories of Ham that he shared years later. Evangelist Ham said people would forget his name. He acknowledged that *Mordecai* was difficult enough. But his last name was easy to remember. He said, "Just remember—my name is the same as the best part of a hog." The evangelist continued, "A woman once heard that and said, 'Oh, now I remember, Brother Chitlin.'"

Ham and his music minister, Brother Ramsey, went to the Corsicana, TX, area. The young E. P. went to help set up the revival tent. The wind was terrible and, try as they might, they could not raise the tent. They tried and failed several times. E. P. said Mordecai Ham gathered the workers together and prayed something like this. "Lord, we've come to do Your work. We've worked hard, but we can't raise the tent in this wind. We know that You are the Master of the wind. We ask You now to calm the wind so that we can raise the tent and conduct this revival. In

Jesus' name, Amen." E. P. said amazingly, they saw the wind almost immediately subside. They then were able to easily set up the revival tent.

Born in Another World

Joe Brumbelow grew up in the country in the days of outhouses, hog-killing in the winter, hunting for deer, wild hogs, squirrels, rabbits, ducks. He grew up in a day of very few paved roads, of public roads where one had to go through cattle gates and cattle guards, family milk cows, chickens, and family gardens. It was day in which men and women of the Old West and the Civil War still were living; when most did not have electricity or indoor plumbing; when horses still were a common mode of transportation. Air-conditioning, TV's, cell phones, computers, and the Internet were far in the future.

Never Again

Joe's aunt, Ella (Follett) Smith, still remembers when Joe visited her house when he was about 5 or 6. She said he declared then that he would never eat another turnip for as long as he lived. He liked mustard and collard greens but hated cooked turnips or turnip greens. At times he grew turnips but only to give away to less-discriminating people. Other than occasionally taking a bite or two of a raw turnip, he kept his youthful vow.

UFO's, Dreams, and Weird Occurrences

Joe once noticed a tabloid newspaper with a photo and the headline, "Scientists Prove This Is a UFO." He thought about it, laughed, and said, "UFO stands for 'unidentified flying object.' All they did was prove that they didn't know what it was!"

Joe was fascinated with the UFO story that was reported out of Damon and occasionally read and watched a UFO story. He knew about the story of the strange lights on Bailey's Prairie. He enjoyed philosophy, near-death experiences, and dreams. Some things exist that we just can't explain. He thought some dreams had credibility; after all, many dreams are recorded in the Bible. He also realized that most dreams have no particular meaning and probably result from what you ate last night. He admitted to having some awfully weird dreams through the years and knew that sometimes people's minds can play tricks on them.

But Joe Brumbelow's feet were firmly grounded in the absolute truth of the Bible—the inspired, inerrant Word of God. He listened with interest to the eerie stories of the day. He didn't have them all figured out. He liked a good story of mystery, but his motto was the same as was B. B. Crimm's banner of years ago, "The Bible Says It, I Believe It, That Settles It."

Or, as Holy Scripture says, "The prophet that hath a dream, let him tell a dream; and he that hath my word, let him speak my word faithfully. What is the chaff to the wheat? saith the Lord" (Jer. 23:28 KJV).

[Brother Joe never would have anything to do, however, with the occult, ouija boards, horoscopes, etc. The Bible forbids it. Joe took that prohibition seriously (Deut. 18:10-14). (For a fascinating dream from the Old West read about Josiah Wilbarger in *Legendary Texians* by Joe Tom Davis, Eakin Press, Austin, TX)]

Don't Blow a Moral Fuse

Joe recalled hearing a church leader years ago speaking in Texas about the need for more pastors in his state. He was from a state that was a pioneer area for Southern Baptist work. This area had a number of mostly small, struggling churches and needed more preachers. The leader then said, "Now, if you've blown a moral fuse, we don't need you."

The Bible makes it clear that God approves of sex within marriage of one man and one woman, but sex outside of marriage is sinful in God's eyes as well as being dangerous and hurtful to yourself and others. (Ex. 20:14; Lev. 18:22; Matt. 19:4-6; 1 Cor. 6:9-11, 15-20; 7:1-5; Heb. 13:4). A few preachers don't realize the hurt they bring on the cause of Christ and innocent people when they act in such an ungodly way. As Nathan said to

180

David after the king had sinned, 'You have given great occasion to the enemies of the Lord to blaspheme' (2 Sam. 12:14). Whether you're a preacher or not, don't blow a moral fuse.

Sour Dirt in Damon

Joe talked about the sour dirt from Damon, TX, that his Dad and uncle took for their health. Joe's brother, Bill, told of how Eldridge Perry Brumbelow and his twin brother, Ailbert Pierry Brumbelow, would get a glass jar, put an inch or so of sour dirt in it, fill it with water, and shake it up. They then would let the water settle and drink a little of the water each day. It must have worked; E. P. lived to be 94.

The story of Damon's Sour Dirt begins with the Karankawa Indians supposedly knowing of and using the sour dirt and spring of sour water. Damon was a part of the land grant given to Stephen F. Austin by the Spanish for him to settle. He brought 300 families from the United States to settle the area. They are called Austin's Old Three Hundred. One of the Old Three Hundred was Abraham Darst, who settled Damon beginning in 1829. Damon, also called Damon Mound, got its name from Samuel Damon, who married Darst's daughter, Lorina. It is the only hill or mound for miles around.

Apparently some time in the 1800s some children were playing around Damon Mound and drank from some of the sour water that had seeped out from the mound. They thought they could make lemonade from it. They returned to their homes to get some sugar and cups. We have no word on how the lemonade turned out, but adults then were curious about the sour water. This led to the famous medicinal waters and dirt of Damon Mound. Some also have just consumed a small portion of the sour dirt.

"Former Brazoria County Judge John W. Damon said he was told that a relative had bottled and sold the sour dirt tonic across the country. 'It was a common remedy,' he said. 'People would pour it into water and drink the water.'" (*The Facts*, Lake Jackson, TX, July 5, 2004; article by Marie Beth Jones.)

Joe's brother, Bill Brumbelow, obtained a sample of the sour dirt in 2000. He had Damon Feed & Seed send it to Amarillo to be analyzed. The analysis showed many of the same chemicals found in multi-vitamin pills today. Lavinia (Bonnie) Brumbelow (Bill's wife) said it was probably the same as taking a multi-vitamin today. Especially for those with a vitamin deficiency in their diet, it must have been a real help.

Helping Young Preachers

Most every preacher can tell you how someone was a tremendous encouragement to them early in their ministry. Preachers need help and encouragement during those early years.

Joe had finished college and was struggling over whether to attend seminary or continue being a pastor. At the end of college he had resigned as pastor at Clegg. Joe, Bonnie and their only son at that time—Steve—moved to West Columbia. Joe needed a job while waiting on his next move. Dow Chemical is a big employer in that area, but it was looking for someone who would be there a while. R. F. Floyd, a great Christian layperson and supervisor at Dow, knew Joe would not be there long but hired him anyway. The job was a tremendous help to Joe and Bonnie for six weeks; then Joe was called to his first full-time church in Houston. By the way, that layperson knew a little something about preachers. His son-in-law was a fellow by the name of James T. Draper, a pastor and now president of LifeWay Christian Resources.

Cast Your Bread upon the Waters

In about 1952 Robert Giesecke was in college. His mother owned a small duplex in West Columbia. When he returned home on the weekends, he would help her with the maintenance. Once, as he worked on the sewer system, the young man who lived in the right side of the duplex walked out to help and to visit. When the work was done, the young fellow asked Robert an unusual question. He asked him if he were a Christian—if he really knew the Lord. Robert replied that he knew the Lord but admitted he wasn't as close to Him as he should be. It really made an impact on Robert that someone cared about his relationship to the Lord. As a result, he got more serious about his Christian life. He never saw the young man again. As life went on, he would think now and then of that chance encounter. Robert could not recall the young man's name and wondered for years who that fellow was.

Fifty years later Robert was reading the obituaries and recognized a name he had not been able to remember. Joe's brother, Bill, later told of how Robert Giesecke, now of Alvin, TX, called him to confirm some of the details. The one who had witnessed to him so long ago was Joe Brumbelow.

In this life we will never know many of the results of our telling others about Jesus.

God Uses Poverty

In his preaching, Brother Joe pointed out that God uses different things to bring us to Himself. He would illustrate by telling of the testimony of Mr. Fink in Damon.

In 1950 Joe was interim pastor of First Baptist Church, Damon. The church had a revival in which Jack Blackwell preached and Roy Cloudt led the singing. During that revival Mr. Fink stood and gave his testimony of how he had been saved just two years before, along with his wife, his youngest son, daughter, Lorene, and her husband, Gilbert Kilsby.

As a child in the 1890s Mr. Fink had arrived from Russia. He stood in Damon Baptist Church and told about his mother praying for her son. Mr. Fink's mother prayed, "Whatever it takes, bring my son to Jesus. If it takes a life of poverty, then use that to bring him to the Lord." Mr. Fink was a diligent worker but had lived in abject poverty in Damon. He told of how in his poverty he finally realized that Jesus was the only way.

The Bible says God's goodness leads to repentance. But sometimes if God's goodness doesn't work, He tries something else.

Chapter 12

The Robin and the Sparrow
Said the robin to the sparrow,
"There's one thing I'd really like to know,
Why these anxious human beings
Rush about and worry so."

Said the sparrow to the robin:
"Friend, I think that it must be,
That they have no heavenly Father
Such as cares for you and me."

—unknown

Three Greek Scholars?
Like ministerial students in college everywhere, Joe made many lifelong friends at UCC. As a little boy I tagged along with him to all kinds of conventions and saw him visit with many of them—friends like Bob Clements, David and Bob Elliot, Ralph Heickman, Wayne Tucker, Gilbert Ross, Clarence Branch, Grayson Glass, Jack Walker, Maurice Morrow, Keith Massey, and many others. He seemed to know everyone.

If anything would have kept Joe from graduating from UCC, it probably would have been Greek. Greek is the original language of the New Testament portion of the Bible. It was a required subject for preachers.

Joe knew the importance of Greek, although he thought some went overboard teaching Greek in their sermons. He used to jokingly point out, "Do you know what John 3:16 says in Greek? It says, 'For God so loved the world that He gave His only begot-

184

ten Son, that whosoever believeth in Him should not perish, but have everlasting life' (the same thing it says in English!)"

Bonnie remembers O. O. Ervin (Joe sometimes called him Double Ought) and Chuck Taylor studying Greek with Joe at UCC. O. O. seemed to be the best of the three at New Testament Greek and tried to help the other two. Chuck would say, "When that mud hole dries up at the entrance to UCC, I'm out of here!" Bonnie remembers hearing comments such as Chuck's saying, "Men, the Lord knows my heart; the Lord knows my heart; and I just can't learn this Greek." O. O. would reply, "Yeah, the Lord knows your knucklehead heart; now let's get back to studying." Somehow they survived and graduated. None of them became Greek scholars, but they all became outstanding pastors and preachers of the Word of God.

Papa George

When O. O. Ervin was pastor at Bynum, he had Joe Brumbelow preach a revival. Revival is a time when you usually pray more and are even more concerned for the lost in the community. The hearts of the people turned toward Papa George. He was an 85-year-old farmer. Where reaching him for the Lord was involved, he was a difficult case.

Most people who accept the Lord as their Savior do so when they are young. That is why children and youth evangelism are so important. The older a person gets, the more set in his ways he or she can become. God can do anything, but the older someone becomes, the chances he or she will get saved decreases.

For 50 years the saints at Bynum had been praying for Papa George. Though some surely thought all hope was lost, they prayed for him during the revival. One night Brother Ervin and Brother Joe spent a good part of the night praying for him. They prayed that God would not let him get any sleep and would make him miserable until he got saved.

The next day Ervin and Brumbelow went to Papa George's farmhouse. He was out working in the hayfield, but his wife was home. She said, "I don't know what's wrong with Papa. He sweated and tossed and turned all night. This morning he had the sheets pulled off the bed." The preachers said, "We know what's wrong. We asked God last night to not let him sleep—to make him miserable until he surrendered to Jesus."

That night during the revival service Papa George trusted Jesus as his Savior. When he was baptized, folks traveled from Waco, Fort Worth, and from all over that part of Texas. They wanted to see the 85-year-old farmer who never was going to be saved—to see him humbly and joyfully follow the Lord Jesus in believer's baptism.

To Whom Are You Talking?

When I was about 4 or 5, Dad asked me to pray at the dinner table. I obviously was young and a little shy and tended to mumble my words. I asked the blessing and concluded with an "Amen."

Dad looked up and said, "David, I didn't understand a word you said." I replied, "I wasn't talking to you, anyway."

A Confirmed Agnostic Meets Jesus

Bryan Nutt lived on the north side of Houston. He was an agnostic; he was not sure that God even existed. Joe visited, witnessed, and reasoned with him. He even later joked with him about visiting the Nutt house. Joe asked Bryan if he knew everything. Bryan admitted that he didn't. Joe asked whether perhaps in the part of knowledge that Bryan did not possess could be the fact of the existence of God. Bryan was at least willing to consider that possibility.

Joe said, "I know you don't believe that the Bible is the inspired Word of God. But suppose it is. Would you be willing to do a test? Read one chapter out of the Gospel of John in the Bible each day. Before you read it, pray something like this: 'God, if there is a God, would You reveal Yourself to me?'" Bryan Nutt agreed to do so.

Nothing much seemed to happen for a while. Bryan later would say, "I began to pray and ask if there was a God, to show me a miracle." God is not obligated and may not be inclined to perform a miracle. But sometimes in God's wisdom and sovereignty, He chooses to do so.

Bryan heard about Evangelist Allan Buchanek preaching across town. He did not tell Joe; he just decided to go hear the evangelist. In that service Buchanek gave his personal testimony. As a young man Buchanek's dream was to become a professional baseball player. But one day he drove by a Sinclair Oil Refinery, at which a gas leak occurred. The gas exploded; Buchanek was engulfed in the flames. All he could do was jump out of the car and roll around in the mud in a ditch to put out the flames. Doctors could not clean the wounds. The damage was so severe, they offered no hope for Buchanek's recovery. Allan Buchanek preached across the country on how God miraculously saved his life, healed him of his burns, and called him to preach the gospel.

Bryan Nutt heard that dramatic testimony and said, "That's what I've been looking for. That's a miracle." The former agnostic gave his heart and life to Jesus Christ. Bryan returned and told Joe Brumbelow, was baptized, and joined the church. Bryan became a faithful member and later was ordained a deacon.

Can't Wait to Look in the Mirror

During the early 1970s Harvey Graham preached a revival for Joe. It was a good revival. Several students from Sam Houston High School attended. That night Harvey preached on hell. I think he scared it out of two or three of them. They confessed their sins and trusted Jesus as their Savior.

Harvey stayed that week in the Brumbelow home. One afternoon Joe saw Harvey sitting in a recliner with his legs hanging between the seat and the footrest. He was browsing through a popular Christian publication to which Joe subscribed. Joe observed him pointing his finger at one or two places on a page.

He then would turn a page or two and go through the same procedure. After viewing this behavior for a while, Joe no longer could contain his curiosity. "Harvey, what in the world are you doing?" Harvey replied, "I'm just counting the number of pictures of the editor in his paper."

I'll let you guess as to which publication. We never had noticed before, but the editor did seem to be pleased with his own photogenic qualities.

The Lord Loves a Cheerful Giver

Brother Joe believed in and practiced giving tithes and offerings. When a special offering was received at church for hunger, disaster relief, missions, etc. Joe wanted to have a part in that offering even when his funds were limited. On the occasion of a special offering Joe reached into his billfold and pulled out a $10 bill and placed it in the offering plate.

When he got home he opened his billfold and was frustrated to discover he had mistakenly given a $20 bill instead of a $10. "Oh, well," he said, "the Lord will give me credit for 20 dollars." "No," his wife, Bonnie, said, "He'll give you credit for 10 dollars, because that's what you intended to put in the offering plate."

(So that no one misunderstands: Joe and Bonnie had a wonderful relationship in the home. The above story, and ones such as "What A Great Testimony" in Chapter 3, do not reflect a bitter attitude. Rather, they reflect the good-natured way Joe and Bonnie sometimes joked with each other.)

Hudgins and Folletts

Joe Brumbelow's mother was Carrie Mae (Follett) Brumbelow. She and Eldridge Perry Brumbelow were married in 1925. Carrie Mae's mother was Mrs. Addie Hudgins Follett, who wrote her life story in 1970. Addie's grandfather was John Longest Hudgins. He was a blacksmith. John L. Hudgins was recruited into Jack Hayes' Texas Rangers and under General

Taylor fought in the U.S.-Mexican War in the 1840s. General Zack Taylor later said of the Texas Rangers, "There is not a coward among them, or a gentleman." John James Hudgins, Addie's father, was born to John L. and his wife Caroline in 1851. As a boy John J. played among the Confederate soldiers at Velasco Fort, TX, during the Civil War.

Despite her Uncle Bill thinking Lon Follett was a "spoilt selfish boy, who did nothing but waste his time and ride good horses", Addie Hudgins married him not long after the great hurricane of 1900.

She tells of several, including herself and Lon, in the Surfside, TX, community contracting typhoid fever in 1901. Addie wrote, "I was pregnant at the time, and Dr. Carlton told us I would be apt to lose the baby any time. I was so weak and rundown. When the baby came about 5 weeks too soon, she was very small and puny. 3 1/2 pounds, but perfect in every way. Thanks to Uncle Alex (as she called Lon's father), having bought and studied a medical book in the earlier days, when the few doctors were so far away and he knew he would have to depend on himself in emergencies, I received the benefit of his patient help in caring for my tiny infant" (from *Retrospect*, by Addie Hudgins Follett). The tiny infant, though not expected to live, was named Carrie Mae. She was to be Joe Brumbelow's mother.

Committees
Definition of a camel: a horse put together by a Baptist Committee.

A Problem of the Heart
In his 40s Joe began having a terrible problem of pain in his shoulder. The pain went down into his arm. Sometimes the only way he could sleep was to lie on the couch and wedge his shoulder and arm into the arm of the couch. The doctor told him, "You have a problem with your neck." Joe said, "It's not my neck that's hurting. It's my shoulder and my arm." The doctor

189

explained that Joe had a pinched nerve between two vertebrae in his neck. They performed surgery on him to scrape away the bone to give the nerve plenty of room. The surgery carried a small risk of paralyzing him, but he emerged from the surgery fine.

Brother Joe used the experience to illustrate our problem before God: "A man has a problem with his hands. 'My hands are doing things they shouldn't do', he says. God says, 'No, the problem is with your heart.' A woman says, 'I have a problem with my feet. They go where they shouldn't go.' 'No,' God says, 'The problem is your heart.' Another says, 'I have a problem with my eyes. They're looking at things they should not see.' God says, 'The problem is with your heart.'"

When we allow God to enter our hearts, forgive us, and make us new creatures in Christ, He changes our hearts. Our hands, feet, and eyes are transformed when our hearts are right with God.

LJ Minister Dies While Fishing

San Luis Pass—A Lake Jackson minister known for his compassion and strong faith died Friday morning while wade-fishing with a friend about a quarter mile from San Luis Pass.

Joe Brumbelow, 72, was fishing at Bird Island when he separated from his fishing buddy only to be discovered about 20 minutes later by another group of fishermen. The Lake Jackson resident was minister of pastoral care at First Baptist Church of Lake Jackson.

Investigator Chris Kincheloe of the Brazoria County Sheriff's Office said the minister was already gone by the time crews with the U.S. Coast Guard arrived. Brumbelow was fishing on the south end of the island without a life jacket.

"There is a cut about 12 feet out," Kincheloe said. "It's quite possible that he stepped off the edge of the cut. We are investigating, but the cause of death won't be determined until we get an autopsy. It looks to be an accident."

190

The minister had recently undergone treatment for a heart ailment, and Kincheloe said a heart attack couldn't be ruled out. The body was sent to the Galveston County Medical Examiner's office for an autopsy. Preliminary results were due Monday.

Although Kincheloe didn't know the minister personally, he said he knew much about him.

"He's one of the faces you always see," Kincheloe said. "It's going to be a tragic loss for the community."

As minister of pastoral care, Brumbelow ministered to people confined to nursing homes, those in hospitals and anyone else in need of special attention. The father of three children, all of whom followed in his footsteps in working with the church, began preaching as a teen-ager, according to the church's web site.

Fishing, hunting and gardening were his favorite hobbies. People who knew him perhaps also know about the large speckled trout he caught last year during a trip to the Texas Baptist Encampment in Palacios.

"He was real proud of that," said Pastor John Hatch, adding that he didn't know how much the precious catch weighed. "I think it grew as we talked about it."

Hatch has many fond words about the man who joined the church's staff in 1998. The community was shocked to hear of his unexpected death, he said. The pastor spent time with Brumbelow's family Friday.

"He had a great heart of compassion for people," Hatch said. "People are really going to miss him. He was really loved."

Edward Webber, associate pastor for First Baptist Church, described Brumbelow as a "very fine person, a very dedicated person who served his Lord." Although he was a part-time minister, Webber said the man he had known for at least 10 years served all he could.

"He was busy in his ministry yesterday," Webber said. "His character was above reproach, and I say that without hesitation."

Funeral arrangements and a memorial service are pending.

(Front page article by Velda Hunter, *The Facts,* Lake Jackson, TX; August 31, 2004. *www.thefacts.com*)

(The next day's paper carried an obituary. His obituary also was listed in the Oct. 18, 2002, issue of the Southern Baptist *Texan.* The autopsy revealed Brother Joe's death was by drowning. When Bonnie was told of her husband's death, she said, "I don't always like what God does, but I trust Him." We don't have all the answers, but we do know that God was with us all each step of the way. Brother Joe is now with the Lord. Many were brought closer to the Lord as a result of his memorial service and homegoing. His funeral service was attended by approximately 700, including about 50 preachers of the gospel. This book probably would not have been written had it not been for the events of Aug. 30, 2002.)

Why Three Kids?

Why did Brother Joe have three children? He explained, "I heard that every fourth child in the world was Chinese; so we stopped at three." (Mart Padgett told of hearing Joe tell a variation of this story with a Chinese woman in attendance. She seemed to enjoy the story as much as anyone else did.)

Revival

Revival—a great outpouring of God's blessing, power, conviction upon a community, people, or nation. A spiritual awakening in which many turn to God.

For several years after he retired from being a full-time pastor, Dad mentioned to us boys that he would like for us to take any of his books that we could use. We took some but were a little hesitant, I think, to take very many.

In what turned out to be the last year of his life, we were going through some boxes of his books. He had a stack of books for us boys to choose from. He paused, then started going back through them and taking some out. "I want to keep the books on revival," he said. He just couldn't bring himself to give them up.

On the Wednesday night before Joe Brumbelow went to be with the Lord, he preached his last sermon at First Baptist Church, Lake Jackson, on the need for revival.

He told of the great revivals of the past. He prayed for revival in America. He told of how some of the old-time preachers believed a great revival would occur just before Jesus would return. Joe was an optimistic premillennialist. To the end he believed in revival.

To All Interested and Uninterested People:

Just a note to tell you of my change of address. I am semi-retiring and moving to my home at 434 Center Way, Lake Jackson, TX 77566. My new phone number is 979-299-6535. This is effective June 1.

I praise God for nearly 40 years of full-time pastoral work and for my wonderful wife of over 41 years who has agreed to move with me; also, for my three boys—one pastor, one evangelist, and one deacon. I never want to stop preaching and will start June 7 as Interim Pastor of First Baptist, Shady Acres, near Brazoria, Texas. I hope to do interim pastoring, supply preaching or part-time pastoring till I am at least 100 years old—also, revivals and Bible studies. No weddings, wedding rehearsals, deacons meetings or committee meetings of any kind! Please keep me in mind for service and, above all, pray for me.

Lake Jackson is near salt water and I plan spending much time in stress therapy sessions with my rod and reel.

God has used some wonderful people and graciously provided us with a lovely home and it is large enough for you to come and visit for a while. Please let us hear from you soon and often. —Sincerely, Joe E. Brumbelow (Letter he sent to friends upon his semi-retirement in 1992.)

About a Preacher's Retirement

Speaking of retirement: a few preachers looked at Brother Joe with raised eyebrows when he announced he would retire.

Some believe a preacher should never retire. Some of those same preachers, however, would retire, without admitting it. They would go into evangelism. They would not preach half as much as Joe did after retirement, yet they were more spiritual than he because they had not retired from the ministry. Joe never stopped serving the Lord and never intended to. He never wanted to stop preaching and telling others about Jesus. His last years were some of his most effective for the Lord. But he was simply being honest in saying that he was retiring from full-time ministry.

Our ministry on occasion will change through the years. And, while this is not necessarily referring to Joe, some preachers have to back off for a while from the stress that pastoring can bring. Joe enjoyed retirement, but he stayed busy serving the Lord and ministering to others.

Getting in the Emergency Room

Brother Joe had a good friend in Dawson who was an alcoholic. James would do well for a while; then he would lose all self-control and drink himself almost to death. On one of those occasions, no one had seen James for some time. Joe went to James' house and found empty liquor bottles strewn throughout the house. James was in bad shape. Joe loaded him in the car and took him to the emergency room in Waco. The emergency room was crowded; he thought James never would be admitted. Suddenly James fell out spread-eagled into the middle of the floor and lay unconscious. Immediately the hospital put him on a stretcher and wheeled him into a room.

Next time you need some attention in the emergency room, remember James' story.

Youthful Mishaps

Like all boys, I suppose, in Damon, Joe had a lever-action BB gun. They look like the Winchester 94 Lever-Action rifles that "won the West." A boy with a BB gun has infinite possibilities.

194

When you open the lever, it cocks the BB gun, compressing air in a cylinder. You then close the lever; it is ready to shoot. Joe wondered what would happen if you tried to shoot the gun with the lever open. He found out. With the lever open, he shot the gun. Apparently the gun shot fine, but the lever slammed shut on his fingers and felt like it almost broke them. He confided in me that he never tried that again.

Bob Glasgow told about when they were in about the second or third grade together. They were in a rhythm band playing sticks and sitting cross-legged on the stage right behind the foot lights. The foot lights were turned on, but one had an empty socket. Joe was curious and stuck his finger in the socket. Bob said Joe later advised him to never do that. (And I wondered why Dad was so afraid of electricity!)

"Once we were out on the school yard during recess. Joe discovered a large wasp nest up in the corner of an outside window. He called Mrs. Blount over to look at it, then told her he believed he could knock it down. He threw a clod of dirt at it and stirred up the wasps. Mrs. Blount had to run as best as she could (she was a large woman). She really fussed at Joe."—Bob Glasgow

Other comments by Glasgow—"Your Dad was an artist at making stink bombs—mostly used, old ink bottles. Sometimes he would put a ladies' bobby pin in a crack in the desk and every now and then you could hear a little twang and no one could tell where it came from. He was not the only one involved in this sort of thing, but he had a certain finesse or originality that was admired by the rest of us."

He continued, "I truly enjoyed being with your dad as a friend and as my (interim) pastor for about a year. During that time it was my delight to be with him on visitation when he led a 76-yr.-old man to the Lord. He was a true soul-winner for the Lord."

The Outhouse
People talk about a house being three rooms and a bath. Joe used to say the house he grew up in was three rooms and a path.

He could relate to the following poem that hung in Joe and
Bonnie's bathroom:

The Passing of the Outhouse
When memory recalls the past and moves to smiles or tears,
A weather-beaten object looms right through
the mist of years;
Behind the house and barn it stood, a half a mile or more,
And hurrying feet a path had made, straight
to its swinging door.

Its architecture was a type of simple classic art,
But in the changing years of life, it played a leading part;
And oft the passing traveler drove slow and heaved a sigh,
To see the modest hired girl slip out with glances shy.

All day the spiders spun their webs to catch the buzzing flies
That flitted to and from the house where Ma
was baking pies;
And once a swarm of hornets bold had built a palace there,
And stung my unsuspecting aunt—I must not tell you where.

Then Father took a flaming pole—that was a happy day;
He nearly burned the building up, but the hornets left to stay.
When summer bloom began to fade and winter to carouse,
We banked the little building with a heap of hemlock boughs.

When Grandpa had to go out back and make his morning call,
We'd bundle up the dear old man with muffler and shawl.
I knew the hole on which he sat; 'twas padded all around,
And once I dared to sit there too,—'twas much too wide,
I found.

My frame was all too little and I jack-knifed there to stay,
They had to come and get me loose or I'd have passed away.

196

Then Father said ambition was a thing that boys should shun,
So I just used the children's hole till childhood
days were done.

And still I marvel at the craft that cut those holes so true,
The baby hole, and the slender hole that fitted sister Sue.
That dear old country landmark—I've tramped around a bit,
And in the lap of luxury, my lot has been to sit.

But ere I die I'll eat the fruit of trees I robbed of yore,
Then seek the shanty where my name is carved
upon the door.
I think the old familiar sight will soothe my fading soul;
I'm now a man, but none the less, I'll try the children's hole.
—Charles T. Rankin (sometimes attributed to James Whitcomb Riley)

The Hairdryer

Remember the Brylcream motto, "A little dab will do you"?
After washing their hair, men applied Brylcream to their hair,
combed it, and had that popular, oily look. Then the dry look
emerged. Men applied Style Gell to their wet hair. When it was
dry, they combed it out and had that dry, stylish look. The problem was—it took a while to dry. About 1970 the dry look was in,
but men's hairdryers had not caught up with the new style. Joe
had washed his hair, applied style gel, but did not have time to
let his hair dry naturally.

Bonnie had a hairdryer—a women's hairdryer. It was composed of the motor unit, a cord to plug in, a hose, and a pink
bonnet attached to the end of the hose. The pink bonnet went
over your head. Needless to say, it did not look quite right on a
man. Joe was in a hurry and needed to dry his hair. He sat down
in the living room, which looked directly out to the front door.
He hooked up the machine and put the pink bonnet on his head
to begin the drying process. He sternly instructed Bonnie and the
kids to give him ample time to hide if anyone rang the door bell.

The last thing he wanted was to be seen with that women's contraption on his head.

Joe's oldest son, Steve, waited for his dad to get settled in. Steve then eased out the back door, went around to the front, and loudly knocked on the front door. He opened the front door to see the hairdryer in three pieces—the motor on the living room floor, the hose and bonnet strewn down the hallway to the bedroom. For a while Joe didn't see the humor in that situation.

A Man from Scotland Gets Saved

O. O. Ervin preached a revival for Joe the first time Joe was at Doverside. They had a great revival but were especially concerned for a man from Scotland—Mr. Robb. Robb had attended the church but let people know that he never had really arrived at a time in his life when he had asked Jesus Christ to forgive him of his sins and enter his heart to be his Lord and Savior. The people prayed for him throughout the revival. On the last day of the revival Brother Joe and O.O. Ervin went to see him. Mr. Robb had not planned to attend the service that night, but because of their visit, Robb decided to do so. He met Jesus as his Savior that night and later became a Sunday-school teacher for junior boys, ages 8-10.

Mr. Robb later would give his testimony and say in his Scottish brogue, "I tried for a long while to think of how I could describe how I felt when I trusted Jesus as my Savior. I could never come up with just the right words. But it was kind of like being in a steam bath, then stepping into a cool, fresh shower."

Mr. Robb continued teaching his boys' class after Joe Brumbelow was called to another church. Several years later Robb died from lung problems. Robb told his wife shortly before he died, "If I had just listened to Brother Joe years ago when he told me to stop smoking, I'd be alright now." Joe returned to preach Mr. Robb's funeral. Mr. Robb's Sunday-school class loved him. The junior boys Mr. Robb taught were honorary pallbearers at his memorial service.

198

That's My Savior!

Mr. and Mrs. A. H. Hall were members of Doverside in Houston when Brother Joe returned to serve as pastor there in 1970. A few days before Christmas the Halls invited the Brumbelows to their home for Christmas breakfast. Joe complimented Mr. Hall's oversized recliner. Later, when Mr. Hall went into a nursing home, Mr. Hall gave the recliner to Joe. Joe's family used it for years.

Mrs. Hall gave Bonnie her recipe for Monkey Bread. The recipe was special to Bonnie not only because it was good, but because Mrs. Hall had written it with difficulty in writing as well as spelling.

Sometime later Mrs. Hall had a severe stroke and eventually was moved into a nursing facility. Joe talked with Mr. Hall about depending on the Lord and not worrying during this time. In his simple, humble way, Mr. Hall replied, "Brother Joe, that's one Scripture that I'm good on. You know, the one that says, 'Be not *worry* in well doing.'" (See Gal. 6:9 KJV for the correct rendering of that verse.)

Mrs. Hall remained in the nursing home and never regained her memory. Mr. Hall's health also began to fail. He asked to be put into the same nursing home, even though they would have to have separate rooms. Brother Joe loved them and visited them often. On one occasion Brother Joe visited Mr. Hall, then went on to Mrs. Hall's room. He entered her room and said, "Mrs. Hall, this is Brother Joe." She replied, "I don't know Brother Joe." "You know me; I'm your pastor." "I don't have a pastor." He then said, "I've just been to visit your husband." "I don't have a husband," and, she continued, "I just don't know anything." Her pastor then said, "Mrs. Hall, do you know Jesus?" For a moment the clouds of her mind rolled away to reveal the brightness of the sun. Mrs. Hall's face lit up, she raised her frail hand, and said, "That's my Savior."

God Saves the Best for Last

At times Brother Joe Brumbelow visited someone in the hospital or in a nursing home who realized things were not going to get better. Health was not going to improve. Brother Joe would say, "I want you to remember one thing. A Christian's best days are always ahead." That simple, yet profound truth brought real comfort to so many.

Friend, if you know Jesus, your best days always are ahead.

Appendix 1

Appendix 1 is intended to give you information on how you can obtain items this book mentions.

LifeWay Christian Resources, 800/458-2772; *www.lifeway.com* or *www.lifewaystores.com* Numerous Christian books and resources. Can order books by telephone or Internet. More than 120 LifeWay bookstores across America. Based in Nashville, TN

WORLD Magazine, P.O. Box 421265, Palm Coast, FL 32142-7579. *worldmag.com* One-year subscription (50 issues) for $49.95. A general news weekly magazine, like *Time* or *Newsweek*, but from a biblical point of view. Editor, Marvin Olasky.

Basics of the Christian Life

A good follow-up book for the new Christian is *Survival Kit for New Christians* published by LifeWay. It is available in children, youth, and adult editions.

Another good book for the new or mature Christian: *The Purpose Driven Life* by Rick Warren.

GuideStone Financial Resources of the SBC (formerly Annuity Board). Based in Dallas, Texas. 800/262-0511. Financial, retirement resources for those in Christian ministry.

Southern Baptist Convention, Office of Convention Relations, 901 Commerce Street, Nashville, TN 37203-3699 USA. 615/244-2355. *www.sbc.net*—Website of the Southern Baptist Convention. Links to all agencies, boards, seminaries, Baptist Faith & Message 2000, of the SBC.

Baptist Press—*bpnews.net* News articles each weekday afternoon. Good source to search archives for particular subjects. Christian news, missions, reports of religious persecution around the world, ethical and controversial news issues.

Southern Baptist Texan—SBTC, P.O. Box 1988, Grapevine, TX 76099-1988. 817/552-2500 *www.sbtexas.com* Free in Texas or a donation of $10 per year. Bimonthly publication of the Southern Baptists of Texas Convention. State and national SBC news as well as general Christian news. One of Joe's favorite papers.

The Biblical Evangelist—5717 Pine Drive, Raleigh, NC 27606-8947. Independent Baptist Publication, Editor— Evangelist R. L. Sumner. One of Joe's favorite writers.

Hannibal Books—publishes this book and many others on missions, family, Country classics, ethical and theological issues, including James Hefley's five-volume classic, *The Truth In Crisis* series, Louis Moore, publisher. *www.hannibalbooks.com* 800/747-0738

Fur-Fish-Game, 2878 E. Main St., Columbus, OH 43209-2698 $14.95 for one year, 12 issues. Outdoor magazine featuring trapping, as well as hunting and fishing. Has historical books, as well as modern books and videos about trapping, etc.

Cumberland's Northwest Trappers Supply, Inc., P.O. Box 408, Owatonna, MN 55060. 507/451-7607 *www.northwesttrappers.com* Catalog with everything you need for trapping.

Texas Parks & Wildlife Magazine, features wildlife, state parks, hunting & fishing. *www.tpwmagazine.com* $19.95 per yr.

Gardening

Texas Gardener Magazine, P.O. Box 9005, Waco, TX 76712. 800/727-9020 *www.texasgardener.com* $21.95 yr.

Womack Nursery Co., 2551 Hwy. 6, DeLeon, TX 76444. 254/893-6497. Mail-order nursery with some of the best fruit trees for the area.

Urban Harvest—P.O. Box 980460, Houston, TX 77098-0460. 713/880-5540 *www.urbanharvest.org* Houston non-profit group researching and teaching classes on the best fruits and vegetables to grow in the Houston area.

Treesearch Farm—wholesale nursery with some of the best fruit trees for Houston area. Based in Houston, TX, but your local nursery must order from them for you.

Brazoria County Extension, 21017 CR 171, Angleton, TX 77515. County extensions have helpful gardening information and classes.

Designer Jewels, 5433 Westheimer, Suite 400 (just west of the Galleria), Houston, TX 77056. 713/623-6996 *www.designerjewels.com* H. R. (Bobby) and Mark Jay Sandler. Longtime Houston jewelers. Bonnie Brumbelow worked for them.

American Tract Society, P.O. Box 462008, Garland, TX 75046-2008; 800/548-7228 Good Christian tracts/pamphlets.

Family Resources (help for the family)

Focus on the Family, Colorado Springs, CO 80995. *www.family.org* Features a wealth of resources for all aspects of family and single life. They publish *Focus on the Family Magazine.*

Ethics and Religious Liberty Commission, 901 Commerce St. #550, Nashville, TN 37203. 615/244-2495 *www.erlc.com* ERLC is a Christian resource for issues such as drugs, morality, family, religious liberty, biomedical ethics, race relations, poverty, gambling, environment, voting, etc. It also publishes *For Faith & Family Magazine.*

King James Only? by Dr. Robert A. Joyner, 760 Tom Mann Road, Newport, NC 28570. Published 1999. ($7 includes postage.) Joe Brumbelow believed this was one of the best books on the King James-Only issue.

Christian Apologetics—An intellectual defense of the Christian faith. Resources:

New Evidence That Demands a Verdict; *More Than a Carpenter* both by Josh McDowell. *The Case For Christ*; *The Case for Faith*; *The Case for a Creator,* all by Lee Strobel. *Who Made God?*; by Ravi Zacharias & Norm Geisler; R. A. Torrey, etc. Available from LifeWay, or most any bookstore can order them for you. You may be interested to know that at least two of the above authors (McDowell & Strobel) were atheists until they checked out the evidence for themselves.

The Bible itself often is the most effective apologetic book for God and Christianity. Many argue against things they think are in the Bible but are not. Read the Bible for yourself. Start with the book of John or Luke. Get a good English translation such as NKJV, NIV, or HCSB.

Sovereignty of God and the Free-will of Man—Joe was a moderate Calvinist. His views were pretty well consistent with the book, *Chosen But Free* by Norman Geisler, Bethany House Publishers.

Books on the Conservative Resurgence in the SBC—*The Truth in Crisis* series, vol. 1-5 by James C. Hefley, Hannibal Books; *The Conservative Resurgence in the SBC* by Jerry Sutton, Broadman & Holman; *A Hill on Which To Die* by Paul Pressler, Broadman & Holman; *Baptists and the Bible* by Nettles & Bush, Broadman & Holman. Available from LifeWay or other bookstores.

Texas Baptist Encampment, P.O. Box 1265, Palacios, TX 77465, 361/972-2717. Where Joe Brumbelow surrendered to the ministry.

Joe Brumbelow grew up at what is now 510 Mulcahy, Damon, TX (GPS: 29 degrees 17.488 N; 095 degrees 44.106 W). It was between the post office and the telephone office. Bull's Grocery Store was across the street.

Masterpieces from Our Kitchen; Favorite recipes from over 50 years experience as a pastor's wife. by Mrs. Joe (Bonnie Galyean) Brumbelow, Lake Jackson, TX. Bonnie's cookbook contains 233 recipes. Included are main dishes, vegetables, deserts, Chinese, Mexican, sugar-free; easy, inexpensive recipes. Every recipe has been personally used by Bonnie and is the best from her experience as a pastor's wife and mother of three boys. To order: Bonnie Brumbelow, P.O. Box 300, Lake Jackson, TX

77562, $13. (Special prices for bookstores and for church fund-raisers.)

Samples of Joe Brumbelow's favorites of Bonnie's recipes:

Chicken and Rice
1 chicken, cut up with skin removed.
1 1/2 cup rice
3/4 stick margarine
3 cups water
1 envelope dry onion soup mix (tested with Lipton's)
salt

Melt margarine in a 9-inch-by-13-inch baking pan. Sprinkle the dry rice evenly over this. Place chicken pieces over rice; sprinkle lightly with salt. Pour water over this. Sprinkle onion-soup mix evenly over all. Cover with aluminum foil. Bake at 375 degrees for about 1 1/2 hours. Sometimes I take foil off and let stay in oven for a little longer just to brown.

NOTE: You also could just use special pieces of chicken rather than cutting up one; just be sure to remove skin. (Can't pull the slippery chicken skin off? Mom taught me this one. Just grab the chicken skin with a dry paper towel. It will grip it and pull it right off.—DRB)

New England Clam Chowder
2 slices bacon, cut into 1/4-inch pieces
2 medium onions, chopped
1 clove garlic, minced
1 rib celery, chopped
1 small green bell pepper, chopped
2 medium sized potatoes, peeled and cubed
liquid off clams
2 cups chicken broth or bouillon
1/4 cup milk
2 tablespoons flour (I usually use a little more)

205

1 large (12-ounce) can undiluted canned milk
1/2 teaspoon Worcestershire sauce or soy sauce
1/4 teaspoon Tabasco sauce
2 flat cans (6 1/2-ounce) minced clams. Reserve juice to use.
2 T. chopped parsley (I use dried)

In large pot, cook bacon until browned. Add onions, garlic, celery, and pepper; cook 5 minutes until tender.

Add potatoes, clam juice, and bouillon. Bring to boil; reduce heat, simmer, covered, 15 minutes or until potatoes are tender. Meanwhile, in bowl combine milk and flour; stir until smooth. Add to chowder; cook 2 minutes or until thickened. Add canned milk, Worcestershire, pepper sauce and clams; cook until heated through. Add parsley.

(I add black pepper and some salt. The Brumbelow men then add a lot more black pepper.)

Note: Omit the minced clams and clam juice and this makes a great potato soup. You might want to double the potatoes for that.

Pecan Pie
1 cup sugar (white)
1 cup white corn syrup
1/3 cup melted margarine
2 teaspoons vanilla
4 eggs
1 1/2 cup pecans
1 unbaked pie shell

Pour pecans in bottom of pie shell. Beat all other ingredients together and pour over pecans. With a spoon evenly spread the pecans. Bake at 350 degrees for about 45 or 50 minutes or until pie seems to be set in center.

(The pecan tree is the state tree of Texas. Visit Texas; we'll teach you the proper pronunciation of *pecan*!)

Salmon Croquettes
1 flat can (7 1/2-ounces) of pink salmon (tested with
    Honey Boy)
1 medium onion, chopped fine
1/2 stack pack of saltine crackers, crushed
2 eggs

Drain as much juice from salmon as possible. Break up with a fork and add all other ingredients. Form in whatever shape you want these (I even have made them in the shape of a fish when the boys were little) and press them firmly together. Carefully lower them into hot cooking oil and fry until brown on one side. Turn to other side and brown. Drain on paper towels.

Note: This is the only thing Joe liked ketchup with!

Mushroom Meat Balls
1 pound lean ground beef
1 medium sized onion, chopped fine
1 cup bread crumbs
1 egg
salt and pepper to taste
1 (10 1/2-ounce) can cream of mushroom soup, diluted
    with one can water

Dilute one can cream of mushroom soup into large saucepan. Mix all other ingredients well and form into small balls. Brown each meatball in skillet (preferably non-stick) and drain on paper towels. After all are browned and drained, add these to the soup which you have just to the boiling point. When all has reached a boil, lower heat and cook, stirring occasionally to keep from sticking to bottom, until the soup has cooked down to a thicker consistency of gravy. I like to serve this with rice.

(Mom also has been known to make this meatball recipe out of buffalo—American bison—and one or two other exotic meats. From Mark or Stephen's taxidermy, hunting, ranching, etc., she has had an assortment from which to choose.—DRB)

Our Own Coffee Cake

1 can flaky biscuits, cut in fourths
1 stick of margarine, melted
1/2 of an 8-ounce box of pitted dates, chopped
approximately 1/2 cup of toasted, chopped pecans
8 packets of artificial sweetener
cinnamon

Dip each piece of biscuit in melted margarine and place down sides of a 7-inch-by-11-inch pan, leaving center strip open. (Reserve 8 pieces for tops.) Sprinkle each row with two packets of sweetener and cinnamon, then chopped dates and pecans. (Toast pecans by putting 1 cup of frozen pecans in a bowl in microwave for three minutes. Stir pecans a time or two. Toasting time may vary.)

Flatten the reserved biscuit pieces. Lay four on each side. Sprinkle each row with remaining sweetener and cinnamon. Bake at 400 degrees for approximately 12 minutes or until browned lightly on top.

Note: Other pans can be used, but you might have to change baking time to adjust to pan size.

(This was one of Joe's favorite breakfasts.)

Appendix 2

Letters to Joe Brumbelow on His Semi-Retirement

In 1992 Joe Brumbelow retired from full-time ministry and immediately began an interim pastorate at Shady Oaks Baptist Church, Brazoria, TX. Arlis Russell, deacon at Northside Baptist Church, Houston, where Brother Joe retired, sent out letters about his semi-retirement. These are a few of the letters sent back to him:

I thank God for you, Bro. Joe. God used you to reach my heart with salvation. I'll never forget that wonderful night of revival at Airway. You posed the question, "When was the last time that you cried for someone to get saved?" and you began to weep. I thought to myself, "Oh, no, here we go again! What an act." But the Holy Spirit spoke to me that night. He said, "Will, he is not acting. He means what he says. His tears are for lost people just like you." Bro. Joe, your tears were not shed in vain that night, for conviction fell and not long after I received Jesus as my Lord and Savior.

—William Passmore, Pastor, Airway Baptist Church, Houston, TX, 1992. (Hendricks Maxwell was pastor of Airway when Passmore got saved. Passmore later became Maxwell's son-in-law and pastor of Airway.)

We spent a number of years under Bro. Joe Brumbelow's ministry—enriched immeasurably by Bonnie, his companion in prayer, service, and love. He has proven over and over his total commitment to serving the Lord in every way that a pastor could. With an unusual compassion and a broken heart, he has loved lost souls into the Kingdom of God, loved wayward Christians back into service and fellowship, and inspired youth and elders alike to devote themselves to evangelism and service to the Lord. He has visited and prayed with the sick, shared the burdens of the troubled, grieved with the bereaved, and encouraged all of these by hope gleaned from God's Word. He has celebrated with those who had reason to rejoice. The Brumbelow home is a place where God is honored, and love and good humor abound. Bonnie is known as the ideal pastor's wife and homemaker, ideal mother and grandmother, champion cook of the world!!!, and a beautiful person through and through. Each of their children could be the subject of another letter, having been brought up "in the nurture and admonition of the Lord."

—Coy and Dorothy Salser, Houston, TX, August 19, 1992.

We met and became friends with Joe Brumbelow through his wife, Bonnie. On those rare times when he came to the office to pick up Bonnie, it was always a delight to just sit and visit with him. We had the good fortune to meet Bonnie and Joe Brumbelow over 25 years ago and have remained friends since that time. The best I can describe Bonnie would be the reply to the telephone call I received from her Corpus Christi future employer who asked me what I thought about Bonnie working for him. I answered that he should be grateful and thank God you are fortunate enough to have her come to work for you. She is a pleasure to work with and we miss her very much.

—Bobby Sandler, Designer Jewels, Houston, TX, August 17, 1992.

Yes, delightful memories: next-door dormitory living (with your pranks), theological developments, ministering together, noting your romancing Bonnie during the revival at Old Ocean, Bonnie's Chinese food, fellowshipping in your home and at conventions, and enjoying David . . . all make our lives happier.

—Dr. Franklin and Barbara Atkinson, Marshall, TX

Joe, we have spent a lot of great times together. Bill and Stony have been a part of those great times that I won't forget. Betty also appreciates the time she was able to spend with Bonnie when they worked together. I think the one thing I remember more than anything else was a time I traveled to the State Convention with you and Bonnie, and the prayer meeting that the three of us had that first night. I listened as you ascended the steps to the throne and really poured out your heart; what an experience we had.

—R. S. (Bob) Baldwin, Pastor, Mangum Oaks Baptist Church, Houston, TX, June 23, 1992.

I first was acquainted with Joe when he was invited to preach Sunday morning at First Church, Old Ocean. When I saw him up on the rostrum, I thought he was ill at ease and I felt sorry for him, but when he stood behind the pulpit and spoke I realized that he was perfectly at ease and spoke with freedom and authority. Joe was interim pastor for us at Old Ocean Second for a while in 1951 where he and Bonnie were married. I have seen him preach with tears running down his cheeks, but he never missed a word. He always preached the Bible and without any apology. The most memorable sermon I have ever heard was his sermon about David and Bathsheba and how God sent Nathan, the prophet, to reprove him and in effect allow David to name his own punishment

—J. I. (Jim) Balkum, July 25, 1992.

While I was pastor in Del Rio, the Lord laid Bro. Joe on my heart as the one we should have to lead our revival. Bro. Joe arrived by train and was a guest in our home. What a grand and glorious week! Not only did we work in Del Rio but in Mexico as well. Since this is a border town, we could get into Mexico to witness to the people and to the ones in the jails. Also, I had a missionary friend who worked there and the three of us did all we could to praise the Lord and witness during this week. This is one of the most joyous times of my life and I thank God for letting us work together.

—Travis Beard, Damon, TX, 1992.

When I think of Joe Brumbelow, I think of a man called of God to preach the Word! Also your tears of compassion have touched many.

—John Brady, Pastor, Woodforest Baptist Church, Houston, TX, August 21, 1992.

We recall the cold winters when we had nothing but natural gas. He and other men managed to get us water. That was a scary time. Bonnie, we are still using your recipes that you shared with us. When any occasion arose sad or glad, you were always with us.

—Neighbors Roy and Blanche Nesmith, Nannie Bob Bruce, Dawson, TX, 1992.

Bro. Joe, I will never forget you. In fact your name is written in my Bible. The night I was saved you told me that just as I have a birth certificate recording my physical birth, I can record that Romans 10:13 is my spiritual birth certificate in Christ. I have never regretted the decision I made that night in your office after a Sunday-night worship service, December 29, 1963. I was baptized the last Sunday you were at Doverside Baptist in January, 1964.
—Charlene Cooper Batts, New Caney, TX, 1992.

Bro. Joe and Bonnie, I remember some years back when you found me all alone in the hospital. Your and Bonnie's visits while I was in the hospital and after I came home (also alone) sure meant a lot to me. Bro. Joe and Bonnie, thank you for being so good to me and may God Bless you. I love you both.
—Grace Carter, Corpus Christi, TX, 1992.

Brother Joe, you will always be my pastor. I probably joined Doverside in about 1959. I was around 13. My family did not go to church. I had attended Lindale Assembly of God a few times with a friend. It was there that I asked Jesus into my heart as much as a child can who has never been taught about God. I know that is when Jesus came into my heart, but I learned what that really meant when I heard your sermons. I walked to church all the time and loved it with a passion. You baptized me a little later. You and Bonnie loved this little odd-ball girl. You taught me what a Christian home could really be. One thing I have never forgotten as I have become an old lady of 45 is that Bro. Joe said his home was heaven on earth. I really never knew anything about this kind of home, because my home was one of alcohol and fussing and even fighting. You grew me so much. Your love for people, lost souls, and missions taught me that love —the love that God is all about. I guess what meant the most to me was one summer I was going to get to go to G.A. Camp in Palacios. This was the first camp I would attend. I was so excited. Laura Evans' mother was to drive us all there. The morning we were to leave it was pouring down rain. Of course my mother would not let me go. I cried and cried. I don't know how you knew it meant so much to me, but somehow you did. The next day you and Bonnie drove me all the way there with your little baby boy, Mark. This was truly the greatest time of my life. It was the first time to live with Christians and learn how to do so and learn the closeness and bonding. I am happy to tell you I serve as president of Baptist Women at First Baptist Porter and sing in the choir. I love my church family. My oldest daughter, Kathy, her husband and three children are very active there, as is my youngest daughter, Natalie, 13.

—Claudia Chaline, 1992.

How the years have flown!! It seems only a short time ago that we were students at dear old UCC. Those memories are so vivid and clear—the Bible classes (remember cleaning out the stables?)—the speech classes—those great history classes when half the time we wondered what in the world he was talking about—the early-morning fishing adventures and so much more. One of the most precious memories to me is that of coming by the service station where you worked and our sharing and praying together. You'll never know how those times blessed and encouraged me. I want to tell you something now that I've never told you before; although I have told many others. You, personally, have been a great blessing and a challenge to me and have been an ideal for me. Your sweet spirit and tender heart, coupled with a love for people, have continuously urged, "FRIEND, COME UP HIGHER." For this, I give thanks to the Father; and I thank you, dear friend. There are so many other things that are brought to mind when I think of you and Bonnie and your hospitality—-your upbeat spirit—-your sharing of your freezer fish —the gracious spirit that seem to permeate your home. For these and a thousand other blessings, thank you.

Brother Tom W. Clawson, Conroe, TX, July 11, 1992.

We lost a dear brother—Norman Cox—while Bro. Joe was our pastor. He was such a comfort to us and all the family. We will always be thankful for his and Bonnie's love shown at times of sorrow. Also we have ate several good messes of fish which Bro. Joe caught. He not only caught them but cleaned and had them pan ready.

—Jack and Cecilia Dunn, Corpus Christi, TX, July 23, 1992.

What a joy it is to recall the years of my association and friendship with you and with my father. I remember so fondly my father's ministry with you through the years. He treasured your friendship and considered you one of his very best brothers in the ministry. He always appreciated your sincerity and sweet spirit. I can also remember the confidence that you had in me when I was just a teenager and allowing me to come to Doverside Baptist and preach for you. Thank you for your confidence in me as a young preacher.

—Daniel Vestal, Pastor, Tallowwood Baptist Church, Houston, TX, June 22, 1992.

I first met Bro. Joe and Bonnie in 1952 when as a student at the University of Corpus Christi. Bro. Joe will always be remembered by those who knew and loved him as the weeping prophet. When I was pastor of First Baptist Church, Donie, Texas, I invited Bro. Joe for a revival. We had a great moving of the Holy Spirit. Bro. Joe asked me to let Stephen preach that last night of the revival services. He did and preached a great sermon. I believe that was in 1968 and that would mean that Steve was 15 years of age. Isn't it wonderful that Bro. Joe and Bonnie have two sons in the ministry and their other son is a deacon? It says a lot about the family's relationship to the Lord.

—Paul Eaton, Pastor, First Baptist Church, Frankston, TX, August 11, 1992.

I remember well our days of pastoring together in the Corpus Christi Baptist Association. I grew to have a deep appreciation for you and your ministry, especially your love for lost souls and your

214

commitment to the Bible as the inspired, inerrant Word of God.

—Bobby L. Eklund, Director, Church Stewardship Department, BGCT, Dallas, TX, July 21, 1992.

You are a friend and fellow servant that has blessed my life. I can never forget the joy of watching you receive people out on the parking lot on Sunday morning. The little children hugging you and their parents' smiles and hardy handshakes thrilled my soul. I will never forget Bonnie leading the Chinese lady to Christ through the literacy program.

—Bill R. Frazier, Director of Missions, Corpus Christi Baptist Association, Corpus Christi, TX, July 22, 1992.

Very seldom does a man arise among us who exhibits, not only in his person but also in his entire family, what it means to devote all to Jesus Christ. You have been such a man across the years. Brother Joe, you are living, walking proof that a wonderful sense of humor can coexist with remarkable saintliness of life. You have inspired so many of us that I cannot begin adequately to say thank you. Those of us across the Southern Baptist Convention continue to give gratitude to God for the impact and blessing that you and Bonnie have been to us all.

—Paige Patterson, President, Southeastern Baptist Theological Seminary, P.O. Box 1889, Wake Forest, NC 27588-1889, June 24, 1992.

Bro. Joe and Bonnie, you came to our church in a time of real turmoil and you began to manifest the love of God, the love of family and sharing of yourselves to put a church back together that had been divided by the works of Satan. You, Bro. Joe, made the statement that if you had known just how bad it was, you probably would not have come to West Heights. I praise God that He showed you that we needed a godly man and wife like you all and that you followed God's leadership and came. So many times I saw you cry over the condition of this church and pray for the Holy Spirit to give you divine power and leadership and it's those times that I will

215

never forget because you allowed God to be your guide. Words could never express my gratitude to you and Bonnie for the great sacrifice that you made while pastoring West Heights Baptist Church. Things that I remember so vivid about you two was your love one for another. I can still see you walk across to the parsonage hand in hand. Your home showed Christ in the way you loved each other and your family and that you told the church many many times of your love for Bonnie. Your true love for God was manifested in your three sons and how they served God from a child even unto now. You do not find men of God today that can preach the whole counsel of God and then live it. I can say with no reservations that Bro. Joe you were that kind of man of God and I praise God for you. You and Bonnie showed homes how they should be in every aspect. One of the things that was so unique about your ministry is that you WEPT almost every time you preached over lost souls and the condition of peoples' lives. Your invitations on Sunday morning were so full of the Holy Spirit until God just drew people to Christ. Thank you for even giving invitations on a Wednesday night and people were saved. Your love for little dirty children that rode the bus touched me and that it didn't bother you to put your arms around them and give them a great big hug. This is just a few of the things that impressed me so about you both.

Bonnie, words could never express the love you showed to everyone and you or Bro. Joe never showed partiality in any way. Of course your good cooking no one could beat, especially Chinese food. I can still taste it. Thanks for being the wonderful pastor's wife that was willing to share your pastor husband with so many who needed him. Your sweet, quiet spirit and willingness to help in any way will always be remembered.

—Lois and Joy Corley, Corpus Christi, TX, 1992.

We had the wonderful privilege of spending some time with the two of you at the SBC in Los Angeles in 1981. We were barely newlyweds at the time. Being around you was a blessing and encouragement as we saw the love and respect you demonstrated for one another, even after so many years of marriage! It is easy to see how our dear friend, David, loves his parents so much.

—Johnny and Kathy Dammon, (now at Fredonia Hills Baptist Church, Nacogdoches, TX), July 9, 1992.

Congratulations on your retirement from pastoring a church, but praise God you told us one time you would never retire from preaching as long as you had breath. We were truly blessed while having you for our pastor. We can truthfully say more than any pastor or preacher we have known, you and Bonnie lived and practiced what you preached. Bonnie, your disciplined life of rising early every morning and reading your Bible and praying is a real inspiration. You are a super cook, especially your egg rolls. Bro. Joe, your love for little children will always be remembered —our grandchildren will never forget you.

—Tinker and Mary Chloe Crisp, Corpus Christi, TX, 1992.

I have known Bro. Joe and Bonnie for a long time. I knew Bonnie before I knew Bro. Joe. My husband, Sport Hargett, our two girls, Winnie Lee and Bernice, moved on a farm next to Bonnie's family in 1942. I still live there. He witnessed to my husband's parents and brother and won them to Jesus, for which we were real grateful.

—Eloise Hargett, Old Ocean, TX, 1992.

I worked in the nursery for several years and my youngest (Little Bill) was with me one night when Mrs. North and I decided to leave the nursery and see the preaching. She had one baby and I had mine. We sat on the back seat and watched a baptism. Bill, being about 3, began to yell, "Mama, they're drowning him", as the preacher put the saved child under. I tried to quiet him and realized I hadn't prepared him for this.

—Ettrice Heron, 1992.

When I received a call from Mark, I began to remember how hard you labored to win me and my family to the Lord. I remember the many times you and Bob Utsey would take me fishing and I would smoke and argue with you over the Bible. But little by little you were showing me the Lord Jesus and not religion. I love you so much for bearing with me and for your prayers over the years. I also appreciate and remember how you helped Bonnie and me in our marriage—even though you pronounced it our funeral, Ha. Bonnie, I will always remember your example and kind words you have always shown us. Bro. Joe, I also remember your tireless trips to visit my brother when he was in the mental hospital. I remember on one of those trips, my mother told you that people who dipped snuff could go to heaven and you told her, they would have to go to hell to spit. Thanks also for your trip to Mexico; the churches there are still going strong with many souls being won to the Lord.

—Bro. Joe and Bonnie Jamison, 1992.

My wife, Joyce, and I first came to know and love Brother Joe while he was pastor at Doverside (1st time). My wife and I had not been married long. Although we were both Christians, we were not in church at the time. Thanks to the persistent visitation of Bro. Alvin Hallmark and Bro. Charlie Law, we got back in church, rededicated our lives, moved our membership to Doverside the first Sunday after the dedication of their new auditorium. The thing that has impressed me over the years is the fact that Bro. Joe not only preached the Word, but he and his family lived it daily. I've always felt you could usually judge parents by the way their children behaved in church. I remember Bro. Joe's boys, instead of misbehaving and cutting up in church, sitting on the front pew, taking in every word their Dad preached. It doesn't surprise me to learn they have all three grown up and become preachers and faithful lay-workers themselves.

One humorous experience I recall, concerning Bro. Joe, that certainly has had a lasting impact on my life was the time Bro. Joe cured me of my worldly foul mouth. After we joined Doverside, I still had a problem with this bad habit. One day as I sat in the barber shop I was engaged in a big, windy story with the barber. I was spicing the story up with a few four-letter words unbecoming to a

218

Christian. Since I had my eyes closed, engrossed in the story, I failed to see Bro. Joe enter the barber shop. Upon completion of my tale and haircut, I opened my eyes and saw Bro. Joe getting his shoes shined at the other end of the barber shop. I thought to myself, "Good Lord, there's the preacher." When I finished I had to pay the shoe shine boy also, so I eased up and tried to pay quickly without Bro. Joe seeing me. Well, Bro. Joe spoke up and said, "Well, Bro. James, How are you today? I saw you when I came in." I replied, "Fine," and thought to myself, "I wish I had seen you then, also." Bro. Joe continued, "I guess I'll see you tonight (this was Wednesday) and I said, "Yes, I'll be there."

Well, needless to say, between that moment and church time I really wondered how much of that story he heard. Bro. Joe never mentioned anything; however, during his dismissal prayer that night he prayed, "Lord, let us lead lives that others may see Christ in us." I felt like crawling under the pew, because I just knew that was for my benefit. The cure took! Years later when I was relating this incident to Bro. Joe, he laughed and said he remembered seeing me in the barber shop that day but did not hear me telling my story. So I guess the moral of that story is, God uses people to make an impact on others' lives, even when they are unaware of it.

—James and Joyce Kirkpatrick, Van Buren, AR, 1992.

It is a delight and a pleasure to have the opportunity to congratulate Brother Joe Brumbelow and his dear wife, Bonnie, on their retirement. I have had the privilege of knowing Brother Joe for many years. It has been a privilege to consider him a yokefellow and friend in the ministry of our dear Savior and Lord. His three boys are a testimony to his and his wife's godly faith and life.

—Richard D. Land, Executive Director, Christian Life Commission (now Ethics & Religious Liberty Commission), Nashville, TN, 1992.

Bro. Joe! Oh, yes, the fisherman! He truly is one in whichever sense. He would stay in those waters all day, i.e. in his days off, and caught all the fishes to his heart's content or to the legal limit, whichever came first. Then, of course, he would complain about his aching bones after the trip to show off how hard he'd worked. I speculated that he enjoyed the complaints as much as the trip itself. Nevertheless, he was a good fisherman. I went with him fishing many times but rarely could I beat him in the number or in the weight of fishes. He probably prayed harder than I did while I was busy singing my Chinese songs and enjoying myself. Well, of course, he is a preacher! Isn't he? On the other hand, he is also a wonderful fisherman for God. Sadness to say, if every Christian shared God's Word with others with such a fervent and urge as Bro. Joe's, this world would have been evangelized in no time.

I worked with an oil company in Corpus Christi in 1981. I moved from Austin and was looking for a church where God had led me. I tried several churches until the second Sunday, when I walked in West Heights. The church was close to where I lived. God's Spirit was moving in that service via Bro. Joe's preaching. I could not but to accept his invitation to move my membership there. I was surprised by God's work and it had been proven that God's will was surely in our midst, more would be said in the following. After service, I was invited to lunch with the pastor and his wife and a few others. That's how I got to know my pastor better. Later on, I was invited to their house for supper and shared with them my experience with the moonies and how God had saved me from going astray. I also shared my vision of Chinese services in Corpus Christi. There were about two hundred Chinese working mainly in the Chinese restaurants, but no Chinese service was available. Many of them had not had a chance to know the Lord. I believed God led me to West Heights because Bro. Joe always had an enthusiasm for evangelism and he had proven to be a great help in setting up Chinese Services in Corpus Christi.

Meanwhile, I traveled to Austin quite often to see my friends. Once, my former Chinese pastor, Rev. Tang, said to me that I might ask my new pastor if I could move in to live with them because I was always working out-of-town. My reply to him was that how could I propose such a thing to my pastor whom I had known for just a few months? However, God was working. One evening, during supper at Bro. Joe's place, Bonnie said to me that she had something to talk to me about. Immediately, I had a strong sense that I knew what she would be telling me about, i.e. I knew she would ask me to move in with them. Before she went on further, I told her I knew exactly what she would tell me and that was exactly what she told me. Amazing, isn't it? Praise the Lord!

Not long after I moved in, we started to prepare for a Chinese ministry. We elicited help from the Southern Baptist Convention, Corpus Christi Baptist Association, West Heights Baptist Church, and Hyde Park Baptist Church Chinese Mission. Rev. Tang flew from Austin after this Sunday service to preach to us. Bonnie helped to start an English class for those non-English speaking Chinese. Thank the Lord that even though the work was hard, there were results. People came to know the Lord and learned some English also. We had at a point students from Texas A&I University in Kingsville to attend our services. However, at the beginning, when things were slow, I was very discouraged at one point because attendance was low. The lowest attendance was zero. Later on, I used that as a maxim to encourage myself, i.e. nothing would be worse than zero. Bro. Joe and Bonnie were then a great help to me. They shared my burden, work load, and worries. They encouraged and prayed with me at all times. Wasn't that God's will in our midst when I accepted the invitation to join the church!

Talking about Bro. Joe and Bonnie, they meant a lot to me. They were like my parents away from home. Their love and care were abundant and floweth over. Bro. Joe was a very caring person. I received a lot of encouragement and help from him. We prayed often and he shared with me his experience. He was a total support for me. We used to visit people together, even the poor and the sick. Bro. Joe was willing to give himself to help others. On the other hand, he was very humorous. When he was cracking jokes, I was unable to keep my mouth shut. I could not help be laughing till my stomach and chest were hurting and my eyes watery. I was introduced by Bro. Joe as our son and before their friends had a chance to respond, Bro. Joe would look right into their quizzical eyes and added, "Don't ask me why! I was away to preach in a revival in that time." Bonnie would then act like she was irritated but was all smiling. In fact, I still have some of Bro. Joe's jokes. Those that I can remember crack up my friends.

Now, about Bonnie, she meant a lot to me also. She was my audience, comforter, care-giver, counselor, help. I had rarely known such a godly couple. She would listen to my ideas, dreams, sorrows, and share my happiness and sadness. She would give me guidance, advice, instructions, her opinion, etc. I talked a lot with her. You would probably find that she's a good audience. In subtle ways, she made me feel like I was someone important and God saved me not for nothing. You might have known that Bonnie would not let anybody washed her dishes because she said she made the mess and she would clean it up herself. In order to help, I told her that I would dry her dishes because I would like to talk to her. Most the time, I sat on the dryer which was next to the sink and talked to her while she was preparing supper. Oh! Those were happy days. I used to joke that I would make myself a tent on their backyard for my wife and myself after I got married, so that I could still stay with them.

—Bennie Lau, Toronto, Canada; 1992.

Brother Joe and Bonnie, You both have been very special to all of our family. You were there at Doverside when I was saved. You were there when I was ordained a deacon and many other special things that have happened in our family. You were there when our girls were saved and when some of our grandchildren were saved. We have been privileged to rejoice together, pray together, and even cry together. We love you.

—Charlie and Ella Mae Law; 1992.

From the time we came to know each other back in the '50s. I have admired and believed in you. I preached the revival at Doverside with Marion Warren leading the music and we had a good time in the Lord together. (Refers to Dawson where he caught the big bass and the one Mark mounted for me.) The revivals you preached for me were always successful and spiritual and a real blessing to me and my people. My pastor, Brother William Passmore, was converted in one of those revivals and now is my grandson-in-law and my pastor. And I'm not leaving Bonnie out of the picture. She really knows how to prepare one of my favorite foods—Chinese food. She is to be praised in the gates for her years of faithfulness to your ministry. Now, as you know already, I have requested you to preach my funeral when I go home to heaven. I told my wife, Evelyn, that when you get through lying about me, to play my tape, and I'm going to sing "The Holy City" for myself. I've heard if you want something done right the way you want it done, do it yourself. So, I'll sing at my own funeral.

—Hendricks Maxwell; 1992. (Several years later, Brother Joe preached his funeral and Hendricks sang.)

On a humorous note I'll never forget the first time we were in your home. You asked me to pull up a couple of chairs and sit down. I was expecting, of course. I also remember being healed of an illness while you were there. You cried because of the touch of God in my life and for what I had been spared. Neal was very honored to serve as a deacon under your ministry.

—The Mays family; 1992.

Brother Joe, it has been my privilege to count you as a friend in Christ for some 25 years. I have appreciated your sweet spirit and your sincere humility. I believe that you are one of the most compassionate preachers that I have ever been associated with. Your belief in the inerrant Word has deepened my appreciation for you also. Bonnie, I have remarked to my wife on more than one occasion what a fine job you both have done with your sons.

—Maurice McLeroy, Pastor, First Baptist Church, Raymondville, TX; August 20, 1992.

It is with mixed emotions that I note your retirement. I already miss your presence in the work of our association. I praise God for the wonderful influence you have exerted in the work of Southern Baptists through the years. I especially appreciate your strong stand on the authority of the Bible as the inerrant, infallible, inspired Word of God. I also appreciate the sweet, sweet spirit that you always exhibit. It is clear to all who know you that you have a vibrant walk with our Master because He shines through you. Thank you for your leadership in Union Baptist Association.

—J. K. Minton, Pastor, Lazybrook Baptist Church, Houston, TX; June 23, 1992.

Bonnie, when my daddy died, you baked and brought two or three big, delicious pies. Maybe you brought other food, too, but this I remember without any effort on my part. Brother Joe, I'll never forget it was you who conducted my daddy's funeral services. You taught the book of Revelation, verse by verse, and I have never before or after heard anyone explain Revelation as thorough as you did. Mark, Cherry, and Daniel are special to Bill and me in so many ways. Mark, as a teen-ager, mowed my lawn. He fixed a roof on a rent house that never leaked after he worked on it. He did it after a carpenter said it could not be fixed. He drove the church bus so senior citizens could attend the state fair and I was one of them.

—-Junell and Bill Moore, Dawson, TX, 1992.

(Brother Joe), you came back when I needed you with Herbert. That was what he wanted; it was so good to know the one who saved him put him away. You and Bonnie have played a real good part in my life. P.S. You also saved Margie Bell, my sister-in-law, and quite a few others I can think of.

–Ida Maude Layne; 8-17-1992. (Brother Joe did not save anyone; Jesus Christ is the only One who saves. But we know what she means. Brother Joe just led them to the Lord.)

I shall always be thankful that God brought you to First Baptist Church, Cypress, where we first worked together. I'll always be grateful that you allowed God to lead you to call me to come to Doverside and serve with you there. Bro. Joe, you taught me so much about ministering with compassion and love and how to keep my spirits up when people sometimes disappointed me. I'll always thank God for your sense of humor. It's always a joy to be with you because I know I'm going to have the opportunity to laugh! Bonnie, I've never known a more supportive and spiritual pastor's wife. Not only were you supportive of Joe but of his staff members, and your words of encouragement always provided the strength to keep on. Thank you for all the WONDERFUL meals and desserts you prepared for me!

—Sincerely, Daniel Jennings; August 6, 1992.

Your sweet spirit, positive attitude, and great ministry have always been a blessing and encouragement to me.

—John R. Bisagno, Pastor, First Baptist Church, Houston, TX, 1992.

My memory of Joe goes back to my high-school days in Damon, Texas. When I heard that Joe had answered a call to the ministry, I was somewhat shocked! I never considered him exceedingly sinful, just tremendously mischievous. It was in January of 1949 when, on a Wednesday night, I, as a 16-year-old country boy, realized that our wonderful Lord was dealing with me in a very special way. On that night, I chose to go to the Damon Baptist Church and behold, guess who was there preaching, but Joe Brumbelow. A sensitive person, Joe talked to me that very night, and I shared with him my heart. We had driven away from the church, but Joe requested that we drive back. We went inside and down to the front, where Joe began praying for me. He said that he knew who could guide a person in what to do in life, and it was so comforting to have someone give me a vertical viewpoint at that time. The very next morning, Joe was right there at my home, continuing to be a witness to me. When I told him that I knew that God wanted me in the ministry, I received another great shock when Joe replied: "You will preach your first sermon next Wednesday night." I did, and that was the beginning of 43 years preaching the glorious message of Jesus Christ. In reflecting on this call, I realize how Bonnie influenced me during my senior year at West Columbia High School. She talked to me, prayed diligently for me, and urged me to allow the Lord to be the number ONE priority in my life. In September, 1949, Joe, his brother, Billy, and his dad took me with them to the University of Corpus Christi. I lived with them and began my first year of college.

—Roy and Joyce Cloudt, Grace Bible Church, Baytown, TX, 1992.

Carol Ann and I are praying for you and your sweet family during this time. You have done a tremendous job over the years and God has blessed you in a great way. Your family is typical of your own faith. Your preacher sons are an immeasurable blessing to hundreds and thousands of others.

—James T. Draper, Jr., President, The Sunday School Board (now LifeWay), Nashville, TN, 1992.

I wanted to write you to express my appreciation for all that you have meant to the Kingdom of God. You have been used of God in an incredible way and have touched a multitude of lives. When I think of Joe Brumbelow, I think of Dan Vestal, Sr., who preached revivals for you. As a young preacher, I attended many of these revival services. God has greatly blessed you with your family and I know that your are so proud of your sons. They speak loud for you.

—Evangelist Freddie Gage, Euless, TX, 1992.

Our first meeting with Bro. Joe Brumbelow was when we moved to the country in Cypress. We knew we were moving way out in the country, BUT our first Sunday there we decided to try to find a church home and we pulled up to this church called First Baptist of Cypress with our two children, Judy and Matt. The driveway led to the rear parking lot and the entrance doors to the church. We were into the driveway with no place to go but around to the entrance of the church, when we discovered the people in overalls, bonnets, wagons being pulled by no less than mules. Our thoughts at this point were that we knew we had moved to the country, but we didn't know just how far out. Needless to say we were trapped at the rear of the church and felt we had to go in. THEN we found

out it was a real old-fashioned day and we relaxed a little. (Brother Joe) was the most sincere, compassionate pastor we have ever had.
—Joe and Mary Hitchcock, Cypress, TX, 1992.

You have served faithfully in a variety of ways through the Union Baptist Association. I got to know you best personally through the work of the UBA Nominating Committee. There I came to appreciate your faithfulness, your easy, quiet humor, and your love for your Lord and this denomination. All of that had an important impact on my life, and I appreciate your willingness to serve.
—Jim Herrington, Director of Missions, UBA, Houston, TX, 1992.

It is hard for me to find words to describe a legend. You have been a mighty man of God who has set an example to those of us who follow you. Your convictions coupled with your love for the Lord, His Word, and people, have been a road map that many of us have attempted to follow. You have been a dear personal friend and I appreciate so much your boldness to stand for that which you know is right.
—Dr. John D. Morgan, Pastor, Sagemont Baptist Church, Houston, TX, 1992. (Brother Morgan called me a few days after Dad's funeral. He said he had gotten word of Joe Brumbelow's death just 30 minutes before the funeral, otherwise he would have attended. He left a message on my answering machine saying that he was praying for a double portion of Dad's spirit to fall on us boys. I don't know about the answer to that prayer, but I appreciated so much his gracious comments right after Dad's death.—DRB)

I served with Bro. Joe for nine months when he served Emmanuel Baptist Church, Clute, as interim pastor and four months during the time he served as interim pastor at Demi-John Baptist Chapel. Bro. Joe was well received by all members of each church. He was a faithful and caring pastor. He demonstrated a pastor's heart and genuine love for the people he served.
—letter Mart Padgett sent to FBC, Lake Jackson, recommending Brother Joe as minister of pastoral care in January, 1998.

227

Appendix 3

The Way to Heaven

Numerous times through the years I heard Dad tell someone how to get to heaven. He emphasized that you could know for sure you are going to heaven. He told of how the book of Romans in the Bible has numerous passages that tell about salvation. That is why these verses often are referred to as the Roman Road.

He not only told this in church. He witnessed while fishing or anywhere and with anyone who wanted to be made right with God and someday go to heaven to be with the Lord.

After Joe went to be with the Lord, someone said, "He never left you without knowing if you knew the Lord." He wanted everyone to know Jesus.

Joe's explanation of the Roman Road of Salvation is for everyone. He explained it something like this:

Romans 3:23 "For all have sinned and fall short of the glory of God."

Sin means to do something displeasing to God.

God says that all have sinned.

We sometimes find someone worse than we are, and compare ourselves to them. God compares us to His own righteousness, and we all fall short.

Romans 6:23 "For the wages of sin is death, but the gift of God is eternal life in Christ Jesus our Lord."

The payment of our sin is death.

Spiritual death is separation from God.

Ultimately sin leads to physical death and hell.

But there is hope. God's gift is eternal life. This eternal life is through His Son.

A gift cannot be worked for or earned. It is free.

But a gift must be accepted, received.

A gift costs the one who receives it nothing; but it costs the One who gives it.

What did it cost God? Look at the next verse.

Romans 5:8 "But God demonstrates His own love toward us, in that while we were still sinners, Christ died for us."

Before you knew God, before you were even born, God loved you and wanted you to be forgiven.

While we were sinners, Jesus died on the cross for our sins. Jesus took our place. If we ask Jesus to forgive us of our sins, He will do it.

Romans 10:9-10 "If you confess with your mouth the Lord Jesus and believe in your heart that God has raised Him from the dead, you will be saved. For with the heart one believes unto righteousness, and with the mouth confession is made unto salvation."

If you will confess the Lord Jesus. *Lord* means about the same as our word *boss*. Are you willing to allow Jesus to be the King, the boss of your life?

God raised Jesus from the dead. On the third day He rose again. That is what Easter is all about.

Believe in your heart. Just repeating words in prayer mean nothing unless you really believe them in your heart.

Romans 10:13 "For whoever calls on the name of the Lord shall be saved."

This verse makes it as clear and simple as you can get.

Jesus died for your sins and He rose again. If you will simply call on Him, you will be saved.

Saved from your sins. Saved from being separated from God. Saved and made a part of God's family.

Joe would ask, "Are you willing to ask the Lord to save you and really mean it in your heart?" If they said *yes*, he would then ask, "Would you like me to pray and you repeat the words out loud?"

He would pray something like this:

"Lord Jesus, I know that I'm a sinner. I believe You died on the cross for my sins. I believe that You rose from the dead and are living today. Please forgive me of all my sins. Come into my heart and be my Lord and Savior. In Jesus' name, Amen.

Joe would ask, "Did you really mean it in your heart? Then you are forgiven, saved, and a child of God. Look again at Romans 10:13."

Joe would then sometimes lead them in a second brief prayer: "Thank you Lord, for saving me. Help me to live for You. In Jesus' name, Amen."

What to do now that you are a new believer:

1. Tell someone who would be glad to hear about what has happened to you.

2. Read the Bible every day. Read at least one chapter each day. Begin in the Gospel of John or Luke.

3. Find a Bible-believing church and attend every Sunday. Tell the pastor what has happened to you.

4. Jesus commanded new believers to be baptized. Baptism is a picture of a death, burial, and resurrection. It tells the church and the world that you believe Jesus died for you and rose again. It also tells them you died to your old life before you met Jesus and now have a new life in Jesus; you've been born again. If still at home, check with your parents about being baptized. Talk with your pastor about baptism. Do so as soon as possible (Matt. 28:19; Mark 1:9; Rom. 6:4; Col. 2:12-13; Acts 2:41-42).

4. Pray. When you read the Bible, it is God talking to you. When you pray you are talking to God. Thank Him for His goodness. (See Basics of the Christian Life, Chapter 4)

Only a Sinner

One of Brother Joe's favorite songs was, "Only a Sinner Saved By Grace." Through the years he had said that he wanted that song sung at his funeral. It was. He was buried in Damon, TX, where he grew up. On his granite gravestone in the Yelderman Cemetery, right next to the Damon Cemetery (1616 Stockwell, Damon, TX), his family had these words inscribed:

Joseph E. Brumbelow
Brother Joe
Southern Baptist Minister
Faithful Loving Husband, Dad, Granddad

June 20, 1930—August 30, 2002
Only A Sinner Saved By Grace

All of us are sinners. Joe Brumbelow's prayer for all who have read this book would be that you realize that while you are a sinner, you will become a "sinner—saved by grace."

"For God so loved the world that He gave His only begotten Son, that whosoever believeth in Him should not perish, but have everlasting life"—Jesus; John 3:16 in the Holy Bible.

"He who believes in the Son has everlasting life; and he who does not believe the Son shall not see life, but the wrath of God abides on him"—John 3:36. Joe would point out the phrase *has everlasting life. Has* is present tense. If you trust Jesus as your Lord and Savior, your sins are forgiven and you have everlasting life right now. You can know that you are going to heaven.

"Most assuredly I say to you, he who hears My word and believes in Him who sent Me has everlasting life, and shall not come into judgment, but has passed from death into life"—Jesus; John 5:24. (John 14:1-6 also tells the way to heaven).

"If we confess our sins, He is faithful and just to forgive us our sins and to cleanse us from all unrighteousness"—1 John 1:9.

Some Basic Questions:
1. Are you a sinner?
2. Do you want forgiveness for your sins?
3. Do you believe Jesus died on the cross for you and rose again?
4. Are you willing to surrender your life to Christ?
5. Are you ready to invite Jesus into your life and into your

231

heart? If your answer is *yes* to all of these questions, you may want to pray the prayer below.

Prayer
"Lord Jesus, I know that I am a sinner and that You died to save me. I believe that You rose from the dead and are living today. Please forgive me of all my sins. Come into my heart and be my Lord and Savior. I ask this in Jesus' name. Amen."

If you have prayed this prayer accepting Jesus Christ as your personal Lord and Savior, please write your name, address, and date below:

Name:

Full Address (Street, City, State, Zip):

Date (Month, Day, Year):

If you have trusted Jesus Christ as your Lord and Savior as a result of reading this book, we would love to know about it.

If this book has been a help to you in any way, please let us know.

Write us at:
Wit and Wisdom
P.O. Box 300
Lake Jackson, TX 77566 USA

About the Brumbelows

Steve Brumbelow
Stephen, oldest son of Joe and Bonnie Brumbelow, is in full-time evangelism. He was born September 12, 1953, in Freeport, TX. He and his wife, Nelda, have two grown daughters: Amy Wall (Amy is married to Jim Wall. They have two daughters:

Courtney and Ashley.) and Lori Mosser (Lori is married to Brett Mosser. They have two daughters: Taylor and Tori.) Steve and Nelda are owners of Pioneer Home Furnishings in Old Town Spring, TX, where they sell Amish handcrafted furniture. When he's not preaching, Steve also raises cattle. Steve served as pastor in Cross Lanes, WV, for 14 1/2 years and also served on the Executive Committee of the SBC. Steve and Nelda live in Willis, TX. He is available for revivals, supply preaching, and interim pastorates and can be contacted at 936/344-9975 or 281/355-0936.

Mark Brumbelow

Born January 11, 1961, in Houston, TX. Married to Cheryl (Cherry), they have three boys: Daniel, Micah, and Jeremiah. Cherry has Homeschooled their boys. They live several miles out of Brazoria, TX. Mark is a taxidermist and a carpenter. Mark has hunted in Africa, Alaska, New Mexico, and Texas. He is a deacon and Sunday School teacher at Grace Baptist Church of Wild Peach, 5050 CR 353, Brazoria, TX 77422.

Joe Brumbelow had a real love for Mark and Cherry's new church and preached there not long before his death. Their pastor, Terry Backen, told at their building dedication that it did not appear the church would have the funds to build. He told of how that after Joe's death numerous people gave to the building fund in his memory and enabled the church, with the help of the Volunteer Christian Builders, to construct its first permanent building.

Mrs. Joe E. (Bonnie Galyean) Brumbelow (and the other Brumbelows) may be contacted at P.O. Box 300, Lake Jackson, Texas 77566.

About the Author

David R. Brumbelow was born May 8, 1957, in Houston, Texas. He graduated in 1975 from Sam Houston High School, Houston. Attended Houston Baptist University and Navarro College, Corsicana, TX. He graduated in 1980 with a B.A. from East Texas Baptist College (now University) in Marshall. While there he served as president of the J. B. Gambrell Society, the school's ministerial organization. He also graduated in 1990 from Southwestern Baptist Theological Seminary, Fort Worth, TX, with a Master of Divinity (M.Div.). While in high school he served two years as a summer missionary at the Baptist Mission Centers in Houston. While in college he served one year as a summer missionary in the state of Iowa as preacher on a revival team.

David accepted Jesus Christ as his personal Savior when he was 5. His dad baptized him at Doverside Baptist Church, Houston, TX. He surrendered to the ministry when he was 9 and began preaching when he was 13. He was licensed to the ministry May 7, 1975, by Doverside Baptist Church. He was ordained to the ministry at Friendship Baptist Church, Beeville, TX, on February 28, 1984.

David has served as pastor in Beeville, TX; Second Baptist Church, Henderson, TX; and, since December, 1991, as pastor of Northside Baptist Church of Highlands, TX. He also has served for more than nine years as Baptist Student Ministry director at Lee College, Baytown, TX. He has taught Old and New Testament Survey at Lee College since 1993 and taught several Bible courses in 1996-1997 at San Jacinto College, Pasadena, TX. He has served in various areas of local Baptist associations and preached the annual sermon for the San Jacinto Baptist Association in 2000. He has served as camp pastor of Preteen Camp, G.A. Camp, and four years as pastor of R.A. Wilderness Camp at Lake Tomahawk Baptist Encampment, Livingston, TX. He is single with no previous marriage. He enjoys outdoor activities such as gardening, hunting (especially his bear-hunting trip with Mark and Daniel in Alaska), fishing, and canoeing.

234

Photo Album

Above: Joe's father-in-law, Tom Galyean, with his mules Buck (left), and Jack. Joe asked Tom Galyean if he could marry Tom's daughter, Bonnie. Tom replied, "I never gave anyone my permission to marry any of my daughters. But if she's going to get married, I guess you're as good as anybody." Joe thought that statement, from Mr. Galyean, was a pretty good endorsement. Tom and Maude Galyean, Bonnie's parents, lived out of Old Ocean, TX, where Tom plowed his 35 or so acres with Buck and Jack.

Joe and Bonnie Brumbelow, July, 1949. First photo taken together.

Joe Brumbelow, 1951.

Above: Joe's father, Eldridge Perry Brumbelow, right, and his brother, Ailbert Pierry Brumbelow, holding the 47-pound catfish they caught in Big Creek on Roy Brumbelow's property. The picture is taken when they were 81 years old, in about 1961.

At left: Joe's grandparents, M.V.B. and Sarah Jane Brumbelow, and their children on their 50th wedding anniversary in 1915.

At right: Joe Brumbelow, age 2; his sister, Myrtle Mae (Brumbelow) Montier, age 6.

Above: The Brumbelow family at Doverside Baptist Church, Houston, TX, 1971. Photo taken by Coy Salser. From left, David, Bonnie, Mark, Joe, and Stephen. Photo at right: At home in Lake Jackson in 1993. Front row, from left, are Bonnie and Joe. Back, from left, are their three sons: Mark, David, and Steve.

Left to right, Myrtle, Carrie Mae holding Bill, E.P. Brumbelow holding Joe.

Above: Beginnings of the Bible Club at Doverside about 1971. Back yard of parsonage behind church at 611 Duff Lane. David in middle, Mark at front right.

236

At left: Joe Brumbelow with some of the locals on a mission trip at La Ciniga, Mexico. About 1972.

At right: Polar bear and Joe Brumbelow in Fairbanks, Alaska, 1974. Photo by M.J. Thompson, Clear, Alaska.

At left: Joe Brumbelow on a snowmobile, Anderson, Alaska, March, 1974. Joe preached four revivals in Alaska.

Joe Brumbelow with his son, Mark, left. Each is with an 8-point buck killed opening day of deer season. The bobcat was killed by Steve Brumbelow. Later that day grandson Daniel killed a coyote. Photo taken by Daniel Brumbelow, Grimes County, TX, Nov. 4, 2000. Steve and David (not present) both began revivals the next day.

At left: Water tower on top of hill at Damon, TX. First Baptist Church, Damon, on other side of the base of the tower. Back of old First Baptist Church building on left; back of new FBC building on right.

Below: New building of First Baptist Church of Damon, TX.

Left: Brumbelow Road east of Damon. Named after longtime resident and Joe's uncle, M.V.B. Brumbelow, Jr.

Joe teaching a Bible Club about 1971.

Old Damon Baptist Church building, Damon, TX. Newer brick building at far right.

Above: Joe preaching at dedication of first building of Grace Baptist Church in Wild Peach, Brazoria, TX, July 26, 2002. Director of missions Olin Boles at right. Water trough, in background beside building, used as baptistry.

Left and below: Photocopies of Joe's handwritten sermon notes, "See That Ye Fall Not Out by the Way."

Order more copies of

The Wit & Wisdom
of Pastor Joe Brumbelow

Call toll free: 1-800-747-0738

Visit: www.hannibalbooks.com

Email: hannibalbooks@earthlink.net

FAX: 1-888-252-3022

Mail copy of form below to:

Hannibal Books

P.O. Box 461592

Garland, Texas 75046

Number of copies desired _____

Multiply number of copies by $12.95 _____

Please add $3 for postage and handling for first book and add 50-cents for each additional book in the order.

Shipping and handling $_____

Texas residents add 8.25% sales tax $_____

Total order $_____

Mark method of payment:

check enclosed _____

Credit card# _____

exp. date_____ (Visa, MasterCard, Discover, American Express accepted)

Name _____

Address _____

City State, Zip _____

Phone _____ FAX _____

Email _____